NEW EMPLOYEE ORIENTATION

A How-To-Do-It Manual for Librarians

H. SCOTT DAVIS

HOW-TO-DO-IT MANUALS FOR LIBRARIES

Number 38

NEAL-SCHUMAN PUBLISHERS, INC.
New York, London

This book is dedicated with much love and respect
to my Mother, Emma, and
the enduring memories of my Daddy, Joe.

Published by Neal-Schuman Publishers, Inc.
100 Varick Street
New York, NY 10013

Copyright © 1994 by H. Scott Davis

Printed and bound in the United States of America

Library of Congress Cataloging-in-Publication Data

Davis, H. Scott.
    New employee orientation: a how-to-do-it manual for librarians/
by H. Scott Davis
        p. cm. — (How-to-do-it manual for libraries ; no. 38)
    Includes index.
    ISBN 1-55570-158-2
    1. Library personnel management—United States.   2. Employee
orientation. I. Title. II. Series.
Z682.35.E63N48 1994
025.5'6—dc20   93-43416
                                                        CIP

CONTENTS

Acknowledgements   iv

Introduction   v

Determining What's Needed   1

Key Participants   23

Anticipating and Handling Problems   37

Prior to the New Employees Start Date   51

Initial Activities and Materials   73

Additional Materials and Follow-Up Activities   95

Overview of Evaluation Methods   105

Participant Input   115

Utilizing Evaluation Results   129

Selected Bibliography   139

Index   143

ACKNOWLEDGEMENTS

Numerous individuals have contributed either directly or indirectly to the completion of this book. The author wishes to express his appreciation to Dr. Ron Leach, Dean of Libraries Associate Vice president for Information Services and Mr. Ron Martin, Associate Dean for Library Public Services at Indiana State University Libraries for their administrative support and professional encouragement; and Margo Hart of Neal-Schuman Publishers, Inc., for her editorial guidance and abiding patience. Margo made my first book experience enjoyable. Maureen Sullivan's professional insight and awareness of the need for a systematic program of new employee orientation for Indiana State University Libraries served as the primary impetus for ISU's program and ultimately this book. Special thanks are in order for the staff of the Department of Library Instruction and Orientation, ISU Libraries, during the period which I was working on this project: my friends and colleagues, Marsha Miller, Nancy Watkins, and Carol Jinbo.

To my wife, Kathy, and daughter, Lauren, thanks to both of you for appreciating the importance of this project and for tolerating me during those times of low productivity and preoccupation, not to mention all those nights I was not at home. And finally, thanks to the entire staff of ISU Libraries, particularly those who have joined our staff since 1989. The program on which this book is based could not have happened without their willing participation in and their candid evaluations of the pilot program and the program as it continues today.

INTRODUCTION

The idea for this book grew out of the author's participation in a special project at Indiana State University (ISU) Libraries. The need for a formal orientation program for all new library employees at ISU was identified by a library consultant who was hired by library administration to review the Libraries' staff development program and make specific recommendations toward improving it. In response to one of the consultant's recommendations, the Dean of Library Services assigned the author the task of researching, developing, and implementing for a two-year trial period a new employee orientation program for the library system that would work with the Libraries' existing organizational structure, staffing, and fiscal situation. In the course of doing so, the author discovered that the orientation of new employees in libraries was inadequately addressed in the professional literature and in actual practice in most libraries. A book on new employee orientations written by a practicing librarian for librarians was needed.

Almost six years have passed since ISU Libraries first implemented its New Employee Orientation (NEO) program. Following the two-year pilot implementation period library administration was not hesitatant in making the decision to continue the NEO program as a regular component of the Libraries' commitment to staff development. To date, more than 30 new ISU Libraries staff members have participated in the NEO program. In addition, some 20 veteran library staff have actively participated in the program through mentoring, a major component of the program. What observable benefits has ISU Libraries derived from its home-grown NEO program? In their evaluations of the NEO program, new library staff have consistently expressed appreciation for the existence of the program and have reported that it was a valuable and worthwhile experience for them as they began their association with ISU. New and lasting work relationships have been formed between new employees and library staff from other departments and units. The consciousness of all staff has been raised about the need of new employees for unique information and to feel personally a part of the library team. Although its impact is difficult to measure quantitatively, the NEO program appears to be a major contributor toward a general feeling of collegiality and *esprit de corps* among various classifications of staff across traditional divisional and departmental lines.

WHY THIS MANUAL?

Consistent with the overall goal of the "How-to-Do-It" manual series, the ultimate purpose of this work is to provide a practical guide to the process of effectively orienting new library employees to the library as a unique and structured organization, in relation to the parent organization or institution. It is designed to present a menu of program options and activities that can be selectively combined to develop a new employee orientation program tailored to suit the needs and circumstances of any library.

This manual is written for personnel librarians and any individuals who, as part of their job responsibilities, must assimilate new library employees into their library's total staff. The manual should also prove useful to library educators who teach courses in library administration and management. While the author's professional perspective on new employee orientations is from that of a medium-sized academic library, the principles and practices set forth here can be easily applied to all types and sizes of libraries without major revision or adaptation.

Finally, orienting new full-time professional staff and support staff is the primary focus of the book; however, practically all the recommended activities and materials described herein could be used with part-time or temporary library employees depending on local needs and circumstances. Likewise, while student assistants are not specifically addressed, most of the activities and materials could be adapted for them.

THE NEED FOR NEW EMPLOYEE ORIENTATIONS

Staff development programs and activities are fairly common nowadays in most libraries. Given the changes that the electronic industries have sent our way in the past 30 years, library staffs in all types of libraries worldwide are in constant need of upgrading and retooling work skills and knowledge. Most of us would agree that the rate of technological change seems to have increased during the past ten years, and nothing suggests that this is likely to subside anytime soon. Few professions, if any, have been more affected by technology than ours.

That staff development is important goes without saying. Recognition of the importance and unquestionable need for continuing, systematic staff development in libraries is strongly supported in the literature. And a review of the literature identifies numerous programs and activities designed to provide training for library staff. When one begins to examine how staff development is typically approached in libraries as reflected in the literature, it becomes apparent that most libraries have addressed the issue of staff development from the standpoint of continuing education for staff. However, when we try to determine just how systematically staff development is approached, it seems that libraries are missing a major component — specifically, when and *how* staff development begin. The most identifiable group of library staff not well represented in the literature on staff development is that made up of new library employees, that staff category where every library worker begins his or her association with a library as an employee instead of a patron.

Any individual in any job or profession usually vividly remembers his or her first day on the job and can recall that weird mix of feelings — excitement, eager anticipation, and a healthy level of apprehension — all driven by a desire to put one's best foot forward. Depending on individual personalities, these typical first-day feelings are quite often tempered by feelings of self-confidence and concerns about fitting in. These feelings among first-day employees are universal regardless of the size or type of organization, be it a large academic library, a small public library, or a huge corporate library.

Research into the literature of business and personnel management substantiates that the first few days and weeks in a new job are critical to the future productivity and job satisfaction of an employee. It is during this period that the organization imprints on the new employee, causing him or her, consciously and/or subconsciously to form opinions about his or her personal relationship with and attitude toward the organization. Given the impressionability of new employees, and fact that first impressions are important in terms of employee productivity and longevity, an organization (in this case, a library) has an obligation to new employees and, perhaps more importantly, to itself to do whatever necessary to assure that new hires' impressions of the organization are positive ones.

Large organizations, such as business corporations and universities, usually provide some type of orientation for new employees. Such programs and activities are commonly administered from the

---

When trying to determine just how systematically staff development is approached, it seems that libraries are missing a major component—specifically, when and how staff development begin.

...the first few days and weeks in a new job are critical to the future productivity and job satisfaction of an employee.

human resources division or office. In the case of a university, new employee orientation sessions sponsored by the university's human resources office are commonplace. Such orientations tend to emphasize the university's health and retirement benefits, issues specific to payroll, and other university-wide policies. They vary in length from a few hours to an entire day. Almost universally, new hires are loaded down with forms, fact sheets, policy manuals, and handbooks. These organization or system-wide orientations might meet the basic goal of providing needed information to new hires, however, their ultimate effectiveness varies widely, and generally, they are inadequate in terms of orienting the new employee to his or her specific division, department, or unit. Further, providing information and assuring proper interpretation of that information are two entirely different matters. Finally, such institutional orientations tend to be rather impersonal since the new employee is not likely to have any significant future contact with the individual from the human resources department conducting these mass orientations.

Continuing with the university example, after attending a university-wide orientation, how is the new employee then oriented to the library as an organization? Granted, supervisors and/or co-workers of a new employee always provide some type of orientation to the immediate work environment (e.g. introductions to co-workers, location of their desk, office supplies, the staff lounge, etc.). After this initial orientation to the actual work space, job-specific training begins, zeroing in on the nuts and bolts of the job for which the employee was hired. Such general work area orientations as a precursor to job-specific training are important and necessary, and all libraries address this need in some way. But when and how does the new employee learn about library-wide policies that are usually much more specific than the much broader university policies? What about the often unwritten protocols in place within a library? An innocent breach of these could be devastating for a new employee. And, finally, how is the individual introduced to the unique and sometimes complex characteristics of the library as an organization in and of itself? How and where does the new employee fit into the "big picture?" How soon we forget those first-day feelings, now taking for granted those things that often often were learned after the fact or after having unknowingly violated some unwritten, yet understood rule (i.e., those things learned the hard way).

As noted earlier, there is an obvious gap in the library literature dealing with the unique circumstances and needs of the new library employee. Some might argue that the lack of library literature is due to the fact that orienting and training new employees are obvious steps, and developing a systematic program for orienting new employees is unnecessary, merely accentuates the obvious, and/or undermines the credibility of front-line supervisors. This argument is tenable only if one also believes that all supervisors within a given library are of equal supervisory competence; all share identical interpretations of all library policies, concepts, and protocols; and all are equally competent at clearly and accurately relaying this unanimous interpretation to each new employee. Case closed!

Luckily, the literature of business provides a considerable body of practical information describing new employee orientation program models and activities proven extremely effective in the corporate world. These can be adapted and realistically applied to a library setting. The business literature also yields the research and other theoretical underpinnings that can serve as a basis for developing sound rationales, goals, and objectives for an effective new employee orientation program in any library. Most importantly, the literature clearly reflects unanimous agreement among personnel management professionals about the value of the new employee orientation concept and the administrative wisdom of actively addressing it.

PROGRAM RATIONALE AND GOALS

The following excerpts are representative of the writings about new employees and the importance of management's recognition of the raw potential and special needs of this group. Collectively, these quotes provide a sound and straightforward rationale for establishing and supporting a program of new employee orientation in any type organization, including libraries:

> ". . . the person who started work this morning is, at least attitudinally, as close to a 'model employee' as you'll ever get" (Posner, 1986, p. 73);

> A new employee "will probably bring to his[/her] first day on the job a heady combination of excitement, enthusiasm, and anxiety" (Kiechel, 1988, p. 274);

"[New] employees want to turn uncertainty into certainty and become part of the organization" (Brody, 1986, p. 25);

"Employee performance is often directly related to attitude, and therefore shaping a positive attitude must begin on the first day of work and continue throughout the first few months" (Addams, 1985, p. 35);

"No [organization] should hire a new employee without a systematic program that exposes the new employee to all aspects of the business the first few months" (Ray, 1988, p. 34); and

Research studies show that new employee orientation programs "reduce turnover and absenteeism, prevent performance problems, instill positive attitudes about the organization, and pave the way for better communication between the supervisor and the new employee" (Reinhardt, 1988, p. 24).

Developing the goals for a new employee orientation program is fairly simple if one generally accepts the basic premises presented in the above excerpts, since the circumstances and needs of new employees in any type of job tend to be rather universal. Naturally, if the goals of two separate new employee orientation programs in two different libraries were compared, there would be some differences between the two reflecting the unique characteristics of each library. However, variations of certain predictable generic goals would very likely be common to all such programs. Presented as a practical guideline, some goals of a model New Employee Orientation (NEO) program in a library setting would be:

- To make all new library employees feel welcome and comfortable as they begin the new job;
- To provide consistent documentation and interpretation of major library policies and philosophies for all new employees and, in the course of doing so, strive to avoid "information overload;"
- To acquaint all new library employees with other library staff and other departments and units within the library system;
- To provide continuing orientation support to all new employees during the initial months of their employment through mentoring and other activities;
- To tailor individual orientation activities/information according to the varying information needs for different positions within the library and, in doing so, to be mindful

of individual differences among new employees in terms of personal experience and educational background;

- To emphasize the new employee's role and potential for contributing to the overall mission of the unit/department, division, and library; and, finally,
- To call attention to the importance of continuing staff development and the library's commitment to staff training, and to emphasize new employees' share of responsibility in self-initiating/communicating staff development needs to their supervisor.

The immediate and long-term benefits of a new employee orientation program may be viewed from two perspectives: that of the new employee and that of the library. The new employee reaps the most immediate benefits by resolving first-day jitters more quickly and being assimilated into the staff fold from day one; i.e., the new employee develops confidence in the notion that he or she does (or shortly will) indeed fit it. The library benefits in the long run due to the greater likelihood of enhanced employee job satisfaction that, in turn, will result in improved productivity and higher morale, an overall decrease in staff turnover, and increased job loyalty. However, the most important benefit in terms of fiscal practicality and cost effectiveness, is that the library will more likely maximize its return on the time and energy invested in hiring and training the new employee; time is money. This is particularly important since increasing automation in libraries has demanded more and more technical training and expertise at virtually all levels of library staffing. This training does not come cheaply, whether the library has a new employee orientation program or not. Like all other organizations, libraries can ill-afford to lose highly trained employees for reasons that might easily be avoided. The NEO program at ISU Libraries is a success story worthy of sharing.

Like all other organizations, libraries can ill-afford to lose highly trained employees for reasons that might easily be avoided.

◀1 DETERMINING WHAT'S NEEDED

In the Introduction we established the organizational value of new employee orientation programs, now let's look at the first step toward setting up an orientation program. That is to realistically assess the existing library structure and environment with the idea in mind of developing a new library-wide orientation program or overhauling the existing one: What is needed in relation to what is realistically possible? What, if anything unique, is currently being done for new employees in the library? And what improvements or followup could be made in any existing orientation activities to assure the most meaningful orientation possible?

ASSESSING THE EXISTING ORGANIZATIONAL STRUCTURE

The feasibility of a new orientation program within a given library is dependent on numerous factors. While all libraries share certain commonalities in terms of organizational structure and staffing patterns, each library is unique in terms of how these factors coalesce. This section identifies issues and raises questions about library structure and environment that should be addressed in order to determine which elements of the "ideal" new employee orientation program should be attempted.

Questions about current library staffing that should be asked include:

> While all libraries share certain commonalities in terms of organizational structure and staffing patterns, each library is unique in terms of how these factors coalesce.

- What is the overall staff size?
- How is the staff classified/distributed in terms of professional/nonprofessional ranks?
- What is the future of staffing in terms of expansion, decreased numbers, or remaining stable for the near future?
- What is the average annual turnover among library staff?
- What are the group dynamics between professional and nonprofessional staff? Is there an amicable, supportive relationship between the two, or is there tension or animosity?

1

Questions about the library's organizational structure and lines of reporting that should be asked include:

- Is there an existing position or department devoted to library staffing and personnel issues?
- If there is no personnel or human resources librarian, is there an existing library department or unit where a new employee orientation program could be placed logically?
- How is hiring and training currently handled?
- In the performance evaluation process for library staff, is any item-specific consideration given to an individual's staff development activities during the evaluation period? Is staff development encouraged or required?
- Might front-line supervisors perceive a new employee orientation program administered outside their management as a threat to their authority or as an insult to their supervisory/training abilities?

Questions about the library administration's position on staff development that should be asked include:

- What is the library administration's attitude toward staff development in general?
- Is there a written library staff development philosophy, policy, or plan?
- Is staff development included in any way in the library's stated goals and objectives?
- Is the administration's commitment to staff development substantiated by tangible resource support?
- What is the library administration's attitude toward the development of a structured new employee orientation?
- Will the library administration positively acknowledge and reward staff members for voluntary participation in a new employee orientation program?

Many of the questions posed above are straightforward, requiring only a simple yes or no, or a checking of figures that should be readily available in any library. Others are much more complex and subjective and will require more thought and analysis. These more complex questions could be addressed through a review of existing written library policies and through candid interviews with key library administrators regarding their professional philosophies on library management. However, all of these questions (and there are doubtless others unique to any given library) should be raised and answered as best as possible in order to proceed systematically with the development and implementation of a new employee orientation program.

HOW SHOULD THE PROGRAM BE ORGANIZED AND WHAT SHOULD IT INCLUDE?

In the process of gathering information about new employees and their initial information needs, be certain to take advantage of existing resources beyond the professional literature. Frequently overlooked, but extremely important, are the professional experts, offices, and organizations usually available in the surrounding community. Examples of such community resources include the personnel or human resources departments of local businesses, hospitals, city/local/state government offices, and public school systems. In communities that have a college or university, there is usually a campus personnel office and a career or job placement center. Information, advice, and input should be sought actively from any of these organizations in the area. Academic institutions offering business degrees are likely to have faculty members who are management, personnel, or administration experts and willing to share their expertise at little or no cost. Appropriate members of the area's civic, corporate, and academic institutions should be contacted and asked if they would be willing to discuss how new employees are oriented into their organizations. If they seem cooperative and willing, you might request an appointment for a visit to their organization to learn more about how they introduce new employees into the work environment. If a community business or public organization has assembled a standard information packet that is given to all new employees just prior to their starting date or soon after their arrival on the job, you should ask if you can have one. If area personnel offices offer orientation sessions for new employees on a regular basis, ask if they would allow observers to the process.

Of course, in contacting area organizations there is the possibility that more than one will indicate that they have no specific program for new employees or that orientations are left to individual supervisors. The business literature certainly does not suggest that new employee orientations exist everywhere in the business world, only that they should. If such responses are encountered, move on and contact another organization, keeping in mind that your institution may have something innovative to share in the near future with those who do not yet recognize the value of systematically orienting their new employees.

. . .be certain to take advantage of existing resources beyond the professional literature. Frequently overlooked, but extremely important are the professional experts, offices, and organizations that are usually available in the surrounding community.

The business literature certainly does not suggest that new employee orientations exist everywhere in the business world, only that they should.

In the case of an academic library giving consideration to the development of a new employee orientation program, if any type of college or university-wide orientation is provided for new employees by the campus personnel office, attend one or more of these sessions since this will help determine exactly what information is being shared with new employees. In the case of ISU, campus-wide turnover among support (nonprofessional) staff positions is such that an orientation program for new support staff is offered by the university's personnel office every Monday morning. The starting date for practically all new support staff at ISU is scheduled for a Monday so all new employees begin their first day of work in one of these orientation sessions. These sessions do not reflect the attendees and where on campus they will ultimately work. New library support staff attend the same orientation session attended by new support staff from academic departments, physical plant, and other service and instructional support units on campus. Sessions run three to four hours, during which time staff members from the human resources office address such areas as health and life insurance programs, payroll procedures, and retirement plan options. All of this information is important to a new employee; however, no library-specific information regarding policies and procedures is provided at this time. (Interestingly enough, while this orientation program is offered to all new support staff at ISU, there is no similar program available for new academic faculty or library faculty at ISU.)

Even though libraries vary widely in size (staff, facilities, collections, etc.), most are usually sizable when compared to other units or divisions of the parent institution. In the case of academic libraries, regardless of campus size, they are usually one of the largest divisional employers within the organization and also have one of the largest budget allocations for personnel and operations (in many cases, second only to the physical plant). Likewise, system-wide library services within some public school systems are elaborately organized, having their own unique procedures, policies, and protocols. Yet many of these large library systems with full-time professional positions devoted to personnel matters are not systematically orienting new employees to the library as an organization. Apparently, it is assumed that library-wide orientations for new staff are being handled by front-line supervisors. However, an informal investigation of just about any college or university campus would reveal a wide difference among departments and units about what is being done in a systematic and consistent way to orient new staff.

STAFF SUGGESTIONS

Without doubt, the single best source of input for determining what is needed for a new employee orientation program is the existing library staff, each of whom was once a new employee. Since they are the most recent members of the new employee ranks, most recent hires among the staff will likely immediately have suggestions about what should be learned early in a job. It would be too easy to assume that since they are the most recent library employees they have the best ideas about what future staff members need. But, "old timers" from all levels and divisions of staff are likely to have a unique perspective on the current library environment since their perceptions are tempered with a sense of where the library has been. Whether they can articulate an organizational philosophy or not, veteran staff have an internalized organizational identity and are, therefore, more likely to think about the orientation concept from an overall organizational perspective than newer employees. But regardless of perspectives, both groups' input is vital to the information gathering process.

Soliciting staff suggestions in meaningful ways so that they can be quantified, interpreted, weighed, and systematically put to productive use involves a variety of information-gathering techniques. Among these are written surveys, brainstorming sessions, and focus groups. In addition to these structured methods, throughout the process of gathering staff suggestions, the individual(s) involved in investigating and developing a new employee orientation program also should actively encourage and provide methods for staff members to provide informal individual input. Given time to think about the new employee orientation concept, some staff members will have additional thoughts or new ideas several hours or a day or two after responding to a survey or participating in a brainstorming session or focus group. Staff members should be encouraged to share such after-thoughts through such informal means as a phone call, memo, or casual conversation with the new employee orientation investigator.

... the single best source of input for determining what is needed for a new employee orientation program is the existing library staff ...

SURVEYS

The most structured and quantitative method for capturing staff input is use of specially designed survey instruments. Several things should be remembered when designing a survey instrument since hindsight following the administration of a survey is too late. First, the survey designer must have a clear understanding of what he or she is trying to measure or find out. Without such an understanding, the resulting survey will prove a waste of time, not only for the designer, but also for the individuals who take the time to respond to it. In addition, the survey designer must already have an idea about what statistical methods will be used to tabulate survey responses (e.g., simple calculation of percentage responses, assigning valences to qualitative responses, or a more sophisticated statistical analysis). Otherwise the data collected will be useless. Other considerations specific to survey design have to do with respondent knowledge of the problem or situation being investigated; respondent demographics; design of individual survey items; and overall clarity of the survey.

The following tips should make survey design easier:

Background Information: The survey should provide an opening statement above its purpose. If the survey is introducing new concepts and a concept might be misinterpreted by staff members, then the concept should be succinctly defined. This assures that all respondents share a common understanding of the issues being addressed by the survey. In drafting a background statement, care should be taken not to bias or prejudice responses by unintentionally suggesting that a new concept is unquestionably good or bad; the tone should be neutral. In the case of new employee orientations there is a reasonably good chance that some staff (particularly supervisors) may not clearly understand the difference between "orientation" and job-specific "training." A brief statement addressing this distinction will hopefully diffuse any anxieties or unintended threats felt by supervisors who confuse the two terms.

Respondent Demographics: There is probably no need to require that survey respondents identify themselves. Besides, respondent anonymity will probably increase the rate of return and will also result in more candid responses to survey questions. However, information about the respondents that might assist the survey designer in interpreting responses should be collected. Specific to new employee orientations, appropriate respondent demographic data would include assigned division (public services, technical services, etc.), job classification (professional or nonprofessional), and years in job (less than one year, one to three years, etc.). The survey designer might also benefit from knowing respondents' specific office or department assignments.

> . . . the survey designer must have a clear understanding of what he or she is trying to measure or find out. Without such an understanding, the resulting survey will prove to be a waste of time, not only for the designer, but also for the individuals who take the time to respond to it.

In small- and medium-sized libraries with comparatively small staffs, however, such information might make identification of an individual fairly simple through the process of elimination.

Demographic-related questions data should be at the beginning of the survey instrument since these types of questions are quick to answer, and respondents will not yet have tired of filling out the survey document.

Survey Design: The survey should consist of a blend of closed- and open-ended questions. Closed-ended, or forced choice, questions require respondents to circle or check a single response or applicable responses from a list of options. These types of survey questions are quick to respond to, easy to tabulate, and are generally easier to quantify and interpret. One notable exception to this ease of interpretation has to do with questions that include a Likert (agreement/disagreement) scale (e.g., 0 = poor to 5 = excellent). In some cases, the surveyor will be interested in the possible reason(s) for extremes in agreement or disagreement. Rather than guess about response extremes, Likert-scaled items could include space for a brief narrative explanation. A simple instruction would ask respondents to "please elaborate" if their response reflects an extreme "in agreement" or "disagreement." In the final tabulation of survey results, this additional information, if offered by a significant number of respondents, would provide the surveyor with information that would suggest taking specific action towards improving or correcting the situation. An important reminder about forced-choice items that incorporate agreement scales — avoid a scale with an odd number of response options. There is a universal tendency for respondents to choose the number in the middle of the scale. Responses that rest in the middle of a scale can only be interpreted as neutral. This problem can be easily avoided by using scales with an even number of response options that forces the respondent to lean one way or the other in responding. (Despite these efforts to force a more interpretative response, there will still be a few respondents who will inevitably invent their own middle ground by creating an invisible rating option in the middle of the scale!)

Open-ended questions require a narrative response, thus requiring more time and thought from the respondent, and more space on the survey. These types of survey questions are the ones most likely to be left blank. Open-ended questions should be carefully worded to focus on a single concept. Ample space should be provided for the response, and an instructive statement should appear somewhere on the survey to "attach additional sheets" or "con-

The survey should consist of a blend of closed-ended and open-ended items.

tinue on back" to accommodate any lengthy responses. Despite their shortcomings, open-ended questions are very important because they provide respondents with an opportunity to express themselves fully and raise issues or perspectives on an issue that might otherwise be lost in a survey consisting solely of forced-choice questions. Open-ended questions also represent an excellent source for well-phrased quotes that tend to reflect the various viewpoints in response to specific survey questions. Open-ended questions are, by their very nature, subjective and, therefore, are difficult to interpret. The simplest means of gleaning collective meaning from these types of survey responses (particularly those asking for a respondent's reaction to something) is to assign an overall valence to each response, i.e., + = positive, − = negative, +/− = neutral. From the final tabulation of responses to these questions, certain basic conclusions can be drawn about general levels of satisfaction or agreement among respondents.

Survey Length/Completion Time Required: There is no hard-and-fast rule or formula to determine the appropriate length of a survey. For a library staff audience being surveyed about new employee orientations, the survey should probably not exceed two to three pages and should not require more than ten to fifteen minutes to complete. If more information is being sought than will fit within these recommended limitations, plan on a second follow-up survey. If two surveys are planned, the first survey should concentrate on obtaining information from staff that might have a bearing on the second survey. For example, an initial survey might ask respondents to suggest activities and materials appropriate for a new employee orientation. A follow-up survey could present the cumulative response to this item as a list of possible "Welcome Package" items and/or initial orientation activities. Respondents could then be asked to rate each item on an appropriateness scale, check all that they believe appropriate, or identify the ten most appropriate items for a new employee welcome package. Further, if more than one survey is used, each should include a number in its header and the background statement should indicate that the survey is "the [first] of [two] staff surveys on. . . ."

Survey Clarity: Instructions for completing the survey should be explicit. Since the survey will probably include a variety of question types, include question-specific instructions as needed. For example, if respondents are given a list of response options, an instructive phrase clearly indicate whether they should check only

. . . the survey should probably not exceed two or three pages and should not require more than 10 to 15 minutes to complete.

one item or all that apply. At the end of the survey, there should be clear instructions about any deadline for completing the survey and to whom it should be returned. Be sure to allow plenty of time for completion and return of the document five working days from respondents' receipt of the survey are the advised minimum response period. After developing a rough draft of the survey, field test it with one or more staff members who have not been involved in its design. Indicate that the purpose of the field test is to receive critical comments about the survey's clarity and instructions, but avoid providing any additional information about the survey other than what is included in its opening statement. After field testers have filled out the draft survey, meet with them to discuss any problem areas and make revisions to the final instrument, under their guidance.

Miscellany: At the end of the survey always thank respondents for their time and input. Encourage them to contact the surveyor if they have questions or afterthoughts about any areas addressed in the survey. If appropriate, share results or a summary of the results through bulletin board postings, memos, or publication in an in-house staff newsletter. Finally, if the rate of return is unacceptably low, send a follow-up memo to everyone thanking those who have responded and reminding those who have not yet responded to do so at their earliest convenience. If the rate of return does not improve, review the survey design for clarity. You might want to contact several colleagues for an objective evaluation of why the response might have been so low.

Two sample staff surveys, each designed to gather input about particular aspects of new employee orientations in libraries, are presented on the following pages. In the interest of space, the response areas on the sample surveys have been minimized.

BRAINSTORMING SESSIONS

In many organizations, brainstorming is a popular method of generating ideas about new ventures or solutions to a problem. Brainstorming, simply defined, is where several individuals get together to generate openly as many ideas as possible about how to improve a service, solve a specific problem, or in this case develop a new program. As a method of gathering staff ideas about a new employee orientation program, brainstorming could be used in con-

---

FIGURE 1-1 SURVEY I: ORIENTATING NEW LIBRARY STAFF

PURPOSE OF THIS SURVEY (Important!!! Please read)

The administration is investigating the feasibility of establishing a new employee orientation (NEO) program for all new library staff. This is the first of two surveys designed to gauge staff reaction to such a program and to gather ideas about what such a program might include. An NEO program would focus on *orientation* to the overall library organization as opposed to task-specific *job training*.

INSTRUCTIONS

In considering each of the items below, recall your own situation during your first few days on the new job. Respond to each item from the standpoint of: "Knowing what I know now, if I were a brand new employee here, I would need to know about... " For items which ask for a narrative response, if sufficient space has not been provided for your reply, continue your response on the back or attach additional sheets as necessary.

Please check all of the following which apply to your current position:

Classification-   Division-   Time employed here-

_____Library faculty   _____Tech. Services   _____less than 1 year   _____3 to 6 yrs.
_____Biweekly staff   _____Public Services   _____1 to 2 yrs.   _____more than 7 yrs.
_____Administrative   _____Administrative

1. Listed below are various topics/documents which could be included in the orientation process. Using the rating scale below, please assign a rating for each item's relative importance **in the initial orientation process**, i.e., the first week on the job.

   1 = very important   2 = important   3 = not very important   4 = irrelevant during first 2 or 3 days

   _____a brief history of the library   _____library mission statement

   _____individual job description   _____library annual report

   _____full tour of the library   _____dept./unit annual report

   _____detailed instruction on the   _____library organizational
        library's automated systems   chart

   _____leave policies/procedures   _____supply requests/procedures

   _____lunch periods/breaks   _____staff/faculty handbooks

   _____performance appraisal forms/   _____introductions to all
        evaluation process   library staff

   _____photocopier training   _____telephone system training

   _____staff phone list   _____dress code

   _____library strategic planning   _____introduction to staff in
        document/5 year plan   immediate work area

--continued on back--

FIGURE 1-1 CONTINUED

_____lunch with mentor,
supervisor or co-worker

_____locker assignment

_____brief orientation to all
library depts./units

_____key request

_____emergency and security
guidelines

_____detailed floor plans
of library

_____tour of immediate work area

_____library brochures/guides

_____orientation to internal library
organizations

_____official library
holidays and hours

_____journal routing request

_____parking information

_____Public Services/Tech. Services
goals and objectives

_____eating place options

Please list any areas not included in the preceding list which, in your opinion, should be included in a new staff orientation program:_____

4. In some organizations "mentoring" is an important part of orienting new employees. **This process involves pairing a new employee with an experienced staff member who serves as a coach/counselor during their first few months of employment.**

   Do you think a mentoring approach would work in an orientation program in this library? (check one)

   _____Yes _____No If "no," why not?_____

   What special considerations might need to be made in implementing a mentoring program for new employees?

   _____

   If a mentoring program was implemented, would you be willing to serve as mentor to a new employee?

   _____Yes _____No _____Maybe

5. Can you think of any creative ways that nonprint media could be used in an NEO program?

   _____

6. How much time do you think will need to be devoted to the general orientation of new staff, and how might the time be allotted? For example, one full day, two full days, three half days, etc.

   _____

7. Please make any other comments/suggestions about new employee orientations not covered above:

   _____

   Please return your completed survey no later than this Friday to the administrative office. You may drop it off in person or send it via internal library mail. Over the next few days, if you have additional thoughts about orienting new library employees, please contact the investigator informally. A summary of this survey's results will be made available in the near future.

   THANKS FOR YOUR INPUT!   [date]

FIGURE 1-2 SURVEY II: ORIENTATING NEW LIBRARY STAFF

PURPOSE OF THIS SURVEY (Important!!! Please read)

This is the second of two surveys designed to gauge staff reaction to the possible implementation of a new employee orientation (NEO) program for all new library employees and to gather ideas about what such a program might include. An NEO program would focus on *orientation* to the overall library organization as opposed to task-specific *job training*.

INSTRUCTIONS

In considering each of the items below, recall your own situation during your first few days on the new job. Respond to each item from the standpoint of: "Knowing what I know now, if I were a brand new employee here, I would need to know about... " For items which ask for a narrative response, if sufficient space has not been provided for your reply, continue your response on the back or attach additional sheets as necessary.

Please check all of the following which apply to your current position:

Classification-	Division-	Time employed here-	
_____Library faculty	_____Tech. Services	_____less than 1 year	_____3 to 6 yrs.
_____Biweekly staff	_____Public Services	_____1 to 2 yrs.	_____more than 7 yrs.
_____Administrative	_____Administrative		

DEVELOPMENT OF A GLOSSARY OF LIBRARY TERMS AND ABBREVIATIONS

Like most other professions, librarianship has its own terminology--abbreviations and terms which have their own special meanings. Some staff development experts suggest the development of a specialized glossary for new employees to introduce them to unfamiliar acronyms and terms they're likely to hear on the job from day one. In developing a specialized glossary, one has to be careful not to let it get too long and cumbersome. On the other hand, in order for a library glossary to be effective, it must be developed for the "lowest common denominator" in terms of past library experience; that is, it must include some very basic library terms no likely to be known, for example, by the new library assistant who has very little or no library background.

1. The development of a **brief** glossary of library terms would be helpful to a new library staff members.

     _____Agree   _____Disagree

2. Listed below are various library abbreviations and terms which could be used as a core list for developing a glossary for new staff. Assuming we were to develop a glossary, review the list, adding any abbreviations or terms which do not appear that you think should be included. Also, if there are abbreviations or terms on the list that you thing should be deleted, draw a line through them.

Abbreviations:

abend	CDAC	ftp	LC	OPAC
ALA	CD-ROM	ILA	LCSH	RLN
ascii	DOS	ILL	NOTIS	SUDOC
BI	e-mail	LAN	OCLC	SULAN

Glossary terms:

barcode	dedicated terminal	gateway	listserv	response time
Boolean searching	default operator	gopher	network	stacks
cold/warm boot	document delivery	internet	online	thesaurus
database	frontend	keyword	reboot	telnet

--continued on back--

FIGURE 1-2 CONTINUED

Suggestions for abbreviations/terms not included in above lists:_____

_____ _____

_____

_____

3. Of the 40 abbreviations and terms listed above, approximately how many could you briefly define in one or two sentences?

_____

DEVELOPMENT OF PROJECT SYNOPSES

Another concept recommended by some staff development writers involve brief written descriptions of major projects taking place in an organization. In our case, such project descriptions would provide a new employee with a general understanding of activities that are having/will have an impact on virtually all areas of library operation. It should be noted that only library-wide projects, not departmental/unit-level projects, are being referred to here.

4. Depending on a new employee's particular position, do you think that the development of **brief** descriptions (1 or 2 paragraphs each) of major library projects would be helpful to him or her?

_____Agree   _____Disagree

5. Listed below are several "projects" currently underway that have short and long-range implications for the library. If brief descriptions of major projects were developed for new employees, can you think of any projects not included on the list that should be? If so, please add them to the list below. Also, if you feel that any of the projects below are not worthy of attention during the orientation process, please draw a line through them.

Major projects:

State University Libraries Automation Network (SULAN)--Phase II implementation.

Continuing development of library local area network and campus local area network.

Development of a library-managed gopher server for Internet access.

Formalized development of library staff training initiatives.

Suggestions for additional synopsis projects: _____

_____

6. Any other comments you would like to make about a library glossary, library projects, or anything else related to the orientation of new employees?

_____

_____

Please return your completed survey no later than this Friday to the administrative office. You may drop it off in person or send it via internal library mail. Over the next few days, if you have additional thoughts about orienting new library employees, please contact the investigator informally. A summary of this survey's results will be made available in the near future.

THANKS FOR YOUR INPUT!   [date]

junction with a staff survey or in lieu of a survey. Whether to use one method, the other, or both will depend largely on such factors as staff size and the amount of time the program developer has. A large staff offers the advantage of more viewpoints on a subject; however, surveys can be very time consuming in terms of initial design and the necessary tabulation and analysis of results. Though less formal and more subjective than written surveys, brainstorming sessions for the purpose of gathering information on topic can be conducted, and the results analyzed, relatively quickly.

Like the survey method, certain considerations should be kept in mind when planning and conducting a brainstorming session. Generally, there are three overriding rules that govern brainstorming:

1. During the session no criticisms or value judgments of the ideas presented by participants are allowed.
2. *Quantity* of ideas generated is more important than *quality* of ideas.
3. No one individual should be allowed to dominate the session; everyone should actively participate.

In addition to these rules of brainstorming, the following suggestions will increase the likelihood of a successful brainstorming session:

Facilitator and Recorder: An individual somewhat familiar with the new employee orientation concept should serve as facilitator for the brainstorming session. The facilitator's primary role is to keep the discussion on track and diplomatically to enforce the rules of the session. The facilitator should have several thought-provoking questions or ideas about the orientation of new employees prepared in advance of the session in case the group needs help getting the discussion started.

One individual should serve as recorder for the group. The recorder should write down every idea presented by the group; complete sentences and overly strict attention to neatness are not necessary. The pace of a good brainstorming session is such that the recorder will have to capture the essence of the discussion through phrases and descriptive key words. If possible, the recorder's notes should be made on a flip chart. A running list of ideas visible to the entire group helps generate new ideas and continuing discussion. Finally, linking the names of individuals in the group notes with their contributions to the discussion would cause participants

A running list of ideas visible to the entire group helps generate new ideas and continuing discussion.

to be reluctant to offer comments about controversial issues. Passive or less confident participants would also hesitate to participate for fear of their comments seeming shallow or stupid.

Given the roles to be played by the facilitator and recorder, obviously they should be identified well in advance of the scheduled brainstorming session so that they can prepare themselves accordingly.

Topics: The session should focus on a limited number of concepts or questions. Very little or no information should be given to participants prior to the session, other than perhaps the purpose—that the session has to do with orienting new library employees. The ultimate goal of the session is to generate creative ideas through spontaneity, fresh thinking, and free association. A possible scenario in a brainstorming session on new employee programs might have the facilitator begin the session by asking participants to think about their very first day in their current job and to recall the thoughts and feelings they had at the time. Participants could then be asked what information about the library did they need during their first few days on the job. Was there information about policies, procedures, or even something as simple as the location of the restrooms that they remember learning the hard way? What information about the library would a new employee who was starting the job today find most helpful during his or her first few days? What kinds of materials (library handouts, brochures, etc.) might be appropriate to include in a "Welcome Package" for new library employees?

The ultimate goal of the [brainstorming] session is to generate creative ideas through spontaneity, fresh thinking, and free association.

Participant Selection: The number of participants should be between six and ten, including the facilitator and recorder. Depending on staff size and the amount of time the program developer has for gathering staff input, multiple concurrent brainstorming sessions might be desirable. Participants should be selected so that the resulting group represents a cross-section of the entire library staff. In selecting participants, some consideration should be given to participant personalities. Staff members who are known to be outspoken, aggressive, or domineering would probably not be good participants since they might stifle creativity and intimidate any of the more restrained personalities in the group. Likewise, staff who are extremely introverted and passive might not be good participant choices since they might be less prone to active participation in such exercises. So as not to appear discriminatory toward the domineering or the passive, it should be noted that both of these types of individuals are well suited to surveys. The domineering types usually like open-ended survey questions and the opportunity to express their opinions, while the more subdued types prefer the anonymity and passive participation afforded by written surveys.

Miscellaneous: The sessions should allow not less than 20 to 30 minutes for the discussion of each issue or question. A single brainstorming session should not last for more than two hours. It is the facilitator's and recorder's responsibility to adhere to a predetermined time limit. Before moving from one issue to the next, the facilitator should briefly review the highlights of the discussion on that issue. This allows participants to clarify earlier responses and also provides the recorder an opportunity to play catch up and fill any gaps in the group's notes. As with written surveys, at the end of the session, the facilitator should thank everyone for their participation and encourage participants to forward any additional ideas that might come to them relatively soon after the session. Finally, a written summary of the results or conclusions drawn from the group's effort should be shared with each participant, and perhaps the entire library staff.

Determining Results: Determining the final results of a brainstorming session is a subjective process. As soon after the session as possible, the facilitator and recorder should meet with the investigator to review the group's notes. A first review should focus on the identification of key words and phrases. During a second review, response patterns and trends typically emerge. Such patterns reflect the collective perceptions of the group about the issues and questions addressed during the session. They are the end products of the brainstorming session and should provide the investigator with insight about the staff's attitudes or perceptions of the issues presented. More importantly, session results will provide the investigator with numerous tangible ideas about materials and activities for orienting new employees.

> Participants should be selected so that the resulting group represents a cross-section of the entire library staff.

FOCUS GROUPS

Focus groups are a common marketing tool in the corporate world. They are facilitated interviews of a select group of participants on a specific issue or issues and are most often used to determine client impressions about a product or service. Focus groups are very similar to brainstorming sessions in that both are group techniques aimed at gathering information. However, for the purposes under discussion here, a primary difference between the two techniques has to do with the composition of the groups. In brainstorming, the group is heterogeneous; participants are selected so the final group represents a cross-section of the entire library staff. Focus groups tend to be more homogeneous in terms of some participant characteristic. Regarding new employee orientations, a focus group would consist of only new employees or, in the case of a library where there is already some form of staff orientation, selected staff members who have gone through the program. Another group possibility would be veteran staff members who have been on the job a relatively long time and who did not go through any kind of formal orientation to the library when they began their jobs.

Another difference between focus and brainstorming groups has to do with the overall nature of how sessions are conducted. As already mentioned, brainstorming is characterized by open discussion, free association, and the generation of as many ideas as possible. Focus groups, on the other hand, are more structured. Participants are asked to react candidly to specific questions put to them about a specific issue. Questions are determined in advance of the session by the sponsor of the focus group (investigator); the list of questions is known as the interview guide. The interview guide should have no more than 12 different questions or topics for discussion. Once all questions on the interview guide have been addressed by the focus group, their work is finished. In summary, focus groups are asked to evaluate an existing situation, whereas brainstorming groups are asked to generate solutions and ideas about a concept or problem.

Information is recorded in a focus group, very differently from brainstorming sessions. In focus groups there is no recorder. Instead, the group's discussion and interaction are typically audio- or videotaped; members of the group are aware that the session is being taped.

Some general characteristics of focus groups and guidelines for conducting a focus group interview are:

Moderator: Focus group moderators present the group with specific interview questions or topics that have been provided by the investigator. The moderator should not be a library staff member or be in any way affiliated with the sponsor's project. This minimizes the likelihood that the moderator will bias the group's responses. The moderator serves to promote interaction among

> [Focus groups] are facilitated interviews . . . used to determine client impressions about a product or service.

group participants and to make sure the group sticks to the topics or questions on the interview guide. The moderator should pay particular attention that participants are provided ample opportunity to communicate fully and explain their responses. This means that the moderator has to be someone capable of rephrasing responses to verify his or her understanding of a given response. The moderator must also be successful in getting participants to be very specific in the reasons for their answers. This requires some skill in asking leading questions of participants as they work through their responses.

Participants: Focus group participants are generally volunteers who respond to a call for participants who meet a particular criterion (e.g., individuals who consider themselves infrequent users of the library). For this reason, the sponsor has little or no control over group composition in terms of personality types. The group should number between eight and twelve individuals, each of whom has some familiarity or personal experience with the topic of discussion. As already noted, a new employee orientation focus group could consist of several types of library employees. Another distinguishing characteristic of focus groups is that participants are usually provided some form of incentive for their participation (monetary or complimentary services or products). The incentive aspect of focus groups is common in business applications since the technique is most frequently used with a group of consumers of a company's products or services. When using a variation of the focus group technique to gather staff input about new employee orientations in libraries, the incentive component would not be necessary unless staff participants are being asked to participate after normal working hours. In such an instance, the incentive could be compensatory time for participants to take at their convenience later.

Conduct of the Session: Ideally, a focus group interview should last as long as it takes to respond to the questions on the interview guide, but realistically it should probably not last more than two hours. The moderator's role as timekeeper requires that he or she make judgment calls about how long the session should last depending on the dynamics of the group.

Interpreting Results: Collecting focus group results is a matter of the sponsor viewing the video or listening to the audiotape of the group's interaction. Valuable interpretive information is gained by the investigator paying particular attention to participants' voice inflection and volume and body language cues (like facial expressions and arm gestures). The investigator should listen for specific reasons for participants' answers and reactions to the items on the interview guide.

Focus group experts, however, warn researchers not to overgeneralize focus group input due to the small group size and to the possibility that the incentive to participate may bias responses. Also, group interaction can be adversely affected by an overly domineering or hostile participant.

For a more detailed discussion of focus groups, see Stewart and Shamdasani's *Focus Groups: Theory and Practice (1990)*.

The information-gathering techniques discussed here should provide a list of numerous activities, materials, and ideas for a new employee orientation program; collectively, the items on the list might be viewed as characteristics of an ideal method for orienting new employees to the library. This ideal must now be evaluated in terms of the realities of the current library situation. Implementation of all the ideas might not be possible or even desirable at first. Any final proposal for the development and implementation of a new employee orientation program within the library must be realistic and practical, as opposed to what would simply be nice.

Any ultimate proposal for the development and implementation of a new employee orientation program within the library must be realistic and practical, as opposed to what would simply be nice.

PROGRAM STRUCTURE

THE GROUP APPROACH VS. ONE-ON-ONE

A new employee orientation program can be structured in several ways, each with varying degrees of formality. Orientation programs for new hires in business and industry tend toward a group approach wherein orientation sessions and activities are scheduled at regular, predetermined intervals and are aimed at all new employees who have joined the organization since the last orientation session. A group approach such as this could be easily applied to any library setting. From an administrative standpoint, the group approach makes program planning much easier and requires less preparation time for each session. Further, in very large libraries with a moderate-to-high rate of staff turnover, a group orientation approach may be the only practical route since one-on-one individualized orientations require considerably more time. Obviously, the group approach is less personal and, out of necessity, more generic than an individualized approach since a random group of new employees would include many different library positions, departments, classifications, and varying degrees of previous library work experience. The result of this mix is varied information needs among all in attendance. Also, for new employees who have joined the staff and have been on the job for a week or more before another orientation is offered, many, if not most, of their first impressions about their new workplace have already been formed. The literature indicates that it would be very difficult to reverse or affect significantly on these impressions.

Despite the fact that a one-on-one approach requires more time of program participants, such an approach is recommended whenever possible because it maximizes the personal aspect of the orientation process and does much to induce and sustain an informal program tone. However, as mentioned earlier, staff size and turnover may make an absolute one-on-one program structure impractical, if not impossible. If a group approach has to be adopted, personalization and seeming informality are still possible through the inclusion of an active mentoring component in the program's design (see Chapter 3).

PROGRAM CONTENT

In addition to ideas adapted from the literature, the basic content of a new employee orientation program should be fairly easy to determine from the results of staff surveys, brainstorming sessions, and/or focus groups. Differences in ranks, classifications, and supervisory/administrative duties of different library positions will be the primary determinants of the appropriate orientation content for an individual new employee. Professional and nonprofessional staff will each have policies, procedures, and forms specific to their classification. Administrative-level positions will likely have information specific to personnel policies and procedures that would have little or no relevance to nonadministrative new employees. Entry-level professional staff who have not yet put the graduate school theories into actual practice will need and require more information and explanation about the day-to-day realities of the profession than the new librarian with several years' experience in another library. Likewise, entry-level support staff with no previous library work experience must be oriented from a different starting point than the new support staff person who already knows what stacks are and understands the basic differences between public services and technical services divisions. NEO content detail and emphases should shift, as needed, for different positions. However, regardless of the job differences among staff, a core content will emerge that is appropriate for all new employees.

PROGRAM TIMELINE

Differences in ranks, classifications, and supervisory/administrative duties of different library positions will be the primary determinants of the appropriate orientation content for an individual new employee.

The most focused and structured period of a new employee orientation program should be the first two to three weeks of a new staff member's employment. Beyond this initial period, structured orientation activities can taper off and become more informal (occasional phone calls, breaks, brief drop-in visits to the new employee's work area, etc., by NEO participants). After several weeks, any additional activities and information can be offered by the supervisor, NEO coordinator, or NEO mentor on an as-needed basis, either when specifically requested by the new employee or when one of the other participants senses the need for further clarification or reinforcement of areas already introduced or topics that have become more important to the new employee's job satisfaction or success as they acclimate over time to the library.

The most focused and structured period of a new employee orientation program should be the first two or three weeks of a new staff member's employment.

Libraries generally have a probationary employment period for all new employees. At ISU, this time period is three months for nonfaculty staff. The ISU Libraries' NEO program duration is arbitrarily set up to coincide with this three-month probationary period. The majority of formal activities and orientation contact among key NEO participants occurs during the first two or three weeks on the job. Subsequent contact is less frequent and very informal. This shift away from structured orientation contact and activities is a conscious weaning that is a logical progression as the recent employee becomes more and more assimilated into the overall staff population—i.e., they are no longer "new."

PROGRAM DOCUMENTATION

Despite its informality, an NEO program should be formal to the extent that there exists a fairly detailed document outlining the particulars of the program. This document could follow the same general outline of this manual, addressing such areas as program goals and objectives, participants, materials and activities, and program evaluation.

In addition to the program document, various other forms and checklists should be developed to facilitate the program's success. Throughout the remainder of this manual, samples of participants' checklists, NEO informational materials, and program evaluation forms are included as practical guides.

2 KEY PARTICIPANTS

The ultimate success of an NEO program requires the active participation of these three individuals [the NEO Coordinator, the new employee's immediate supervisor, and peer level mentor], as well as active support from the library administration.

Aside from the obvious participant, the new employee, an orientation program must include a coordinating individual or committee and the immediate supervisor of the new employee. The use of peer-level mentors in an NEO program can also be very effective toward accomplishing program goals. The ultimate success of an NEO program requires the active participation of these three individuals, as well as active support from library administration.

In larger libraries a new employee orientation program clearly would fall within the domain of the library's personnel or human resources department. In libraries without personnel departments or personnel librarians, the administrative structure should be analyzed to determine if there is an existing department or unit that would provide a logical home for an NEO program. Most libraries have a unit, department, or one or more individuals assigned to user instruction. Expanding on the concept of user instruction to include staff orientation, the user education unit would be one seemingly logical place for the program. If the program can be placed with those in charge of the overall library instruction program, one person in that department could be assigned responsibility for overall coordination of the program. Having one individual responsible for orientation activities better ensures consistency in the information received by all new library employees.

Another way to administer an NEO program would be to include it as a primary responsibility of a library staff development committee. In addition to coordinating an NEO program, this committee could serve in an advisory capacity to library administration on broader, on-going training and development issues for the entire library staff. This arrangement offers the advantage of in numbers and collective creativity from members of the group. Assuming that there is an affable relationship between the various staff classifications (professional/non-professional), another notable advantage to staff development committee coordination is that all levels of staff could be represented (i.e., public and technical services, professional and support staff, etc.). The primary disadvantage of committee coordination of an NEO program is that committees often have a tendency to slow a process down, particularly when trying to implement a brand new program or service, since decision-making and action require some level of group consensus. This usually introduces the inevitable time delays brought on by sometimes lengthy meetings and discussions. Also, if members of a staff development committee rotate specific duties and responsibilities among themselves, there is a greater likelihood of program inconsistency in terms of when and how certain information are interpreted and presented to new employees. Since one of the goals of an NEO program should be the assurance of consistent coverage and interpretation of library-wide policies and procedures, committee coordination may be the least attractive option for where to house an NEO program administratively.

For the remainder of this manual, assume that a NEO coordinator is one individual assigned to coordinate the program; however, duties attributed to an individual NEO coordinator could, with modification, be handled by a committee. Further, even if a single individual is pressed into service as NEO program coordinator, a staff development committee could still serve an important function, as noted earlier, on broader staff development issues, including the review and evaluation of an NEO program.

THE NEO COORDINATOR

The NEO coordinator oversees the general library orientation for all new employees. The coordinator should not be viewed as someone who *takes over* supervisors' responsibilities for job training but rather as someone who assists supervisors by having a systematic means of covering certain essential new employee information. There is a fundamental difference between job-specific *training* and *orienting* a new employee to the overall organization. The operative word in understanding the role of this individual is *coordinator.* Another descriptor aptly attributed to the NEO coordinator is *facilitator,* since one of his or her primary responsibilities is to facilitate communications and interaction between the new employee, other staff, and the new employee's supervisor during the new employee's initial weeks on the job.

The NEO coordinator should be an individual with broad library experience, good interpersonal and communication skills (both written and verbal), and experience in program coordination. Given the instructional nature of the NEO program concept, teaching experience would be advantageous, as would experience in staff development and/or personnel management.

Duties and responsibilities of the NEO coordinator might include:

The coordinator should not be viewed as someone who "takes over" supervisors' responsibilities for job training.

- Developing and maintaining a master NEO checklist;
- Coordinating the development, production, and revision of major library project descriptions;
- Coordinating and conducting training workshops for NEO mentors;
- Coordinating the overall orientation schedule and involvement of others in the orientation process; and
- Coordinating the production of a new employee welcome package of library information for distribution to the new employee on the first day; keeping the welcome package up to date.

In conjunction with the new employee's immediate supervisor, the NEO Coordinator:

- Reviews standard orientation checklists for the immediate supervisor and the NEO mentor;
- Determines, as appropriate, any special orientation activities for the specific position; and
- Assists in the selection of an NEO mentor.

The NEO coordinator, in providing a general overview of the NEO program to the new employee:

- Explains to the new employee the purposes/goals of the NEO program in relation to the library's and parent institution's overall staff development philosophy;
- Explains to the new employee his or her responsibilities in the orientation/staff development processes (i.e., initiates questions, read materials that are emphasized, and communicates future development needs);
- Interprets certain library-wide policies to the new employee (e.g. emergency and security guidelines, library calendar, in-house publications, and organizational chart);
- Arrange for introductions/recognition of new library employees at various library-wide functions (e.g., Christmas party and all-staff meetings);
- Monitors the mentor/new employee relationship throughout the orientation period;
- Makes follow-up contact with each new employee after a specified period to check on progress, need for further assistance, etc.;
- Coordinates formative and summative evaluations of the NEO program via written input from new employees, im-

mediate supervisors, mentors and others involved in the process; sharing evaluation results with library administration, staff, and faculty; and synthesizing evaluation input to determine needed program revisions;

- Based on evaluation input and in cooperation with the library administration, coordinates NEO program revision;
- Serves as the NEO program liaison to appropriate library committees;
- Maintains appropriate communications with the library administration regarding the progress/problems of the NEO program; and
- Maintains appropriate contact with the institutional personnel offices regarding institution-wide changes that might impact on the content of the library's NEO program.

Checklists provide a practical organizational tool for conducting a sequential task or assignment over an extended period of time. Development of checklists for all NEO participants will significantly improve the likelihood that everyone fulfills his or her role in the NEO process. Checklists should provide a chronological sequence of major activities without being too broad or too detailed. Remember that checklists are designed to make the participants' jobs easier, not more complicated because of bureaucratic paperwork. They should include space for participants to record comments and make notes about things that happened during the orientation process that may assist the NEO Coordinator in the on-going revision and improvement of the program. The following NEO Coordinator's Checklist is presented as a model. As with the sample surveys in Chapter 1, space for narrative responses and comments have been minimized here. NEO checklists for immediate supervisors and mentors are included in subsequent sections that discuss the roles of these individuals in the NEO process.

Development of checklists for all NEO participants will significantly improve the likelihood that everyone will fulfill their role in the NEO process.

IMMEDIATE SUPERVISORS

Since the responsibility for a new employee's initial orientation and job-specific training has traditionally fallen on his or her immediate supervisor, it is essential that the supervisor be actively involved in a structured new employee orientation program. Undoubtedly, there are many exceedingly competent library supervisors who do

---

FIGURE 2-1 NEO COORDINATOR'S CHECKLIST

New Employee:_____ Start Date:_____

Position:_____

Library Dept.:_____ Phone No.:_____

Immed. Supervisor:_____ Phone/e-mail:_____

Mentor:_____ Phone/e-mail:_____

GENERAL INSTRUCTIONS

Upon completion of each activity on the following checklist, record the date completed. Use N/A for any activity which does not apply to this particular orientation. An "Other" category has been included in each section of the checklist so that activities unique to the new employee's position may be noted.

I. ACTIVITIES PRIOR TO NEW EMPLOYEE'S STARTING DATE

_____ set up NEO documentation file specific to the new employee; get their home address/phone no.

_____ confirm new employee's starting date (verify with administrative office and immediate supervisor)

_____ initiate "Welcome Letter;" mail one week prior to starting date; copy to supervisor and mentor

_____ schedule meeting with new employee's immediate supervisor; during meeting:

_____ seek supervisor's input regarding the new employee's background, i.e., education, work history, personality, special interests, etc.; develop general summary for sharing with mentor

_____ review orientation content and supervisor's role in NEO process; refine supervisor's checklist as necessary

_____ based on requirements of the position, determine possible need for special presenters; contact special presenters, as appropriate, for scheduling

_____ select and rank order mentor candidates

_____ seek mentor candidate's supervisor's approval for participation

_____ meet with mentor to review mentor role; review NEO content and refine mentor checklist as necessary; if possible, provide mentor with background information regarding new employee's work history, special interests, etc.

_____ coordinate scheduling of orientation activities as agreed upon with supervisor and mentor, i.e., Coordinator's initial meeting(s) with new employee, introduction to mentor, etc.

_____ arrange for in-house announcement to staff of new employee's arrival; identify position

_____ assemble "Welcome Package" containing information consistent with new employee's position and previous library work experience

_____ project evaluation dates on coordinator's personal calendar:

_____ new employee evaluation I (approximately 3 weeks after start date)

--continued on back--

FIGURE 2-1 CONTINUED

_____ new employee evaluation II, mentor evaluation, and immediate supervisor's evaluation (approximately 3 months after start date)

_____ Other (elaborate):_____

Comments:_____

II. INITIAL MEETING WITH NEW EMPLOYEE (preferably first day on the job)

_____ provide brief history of NEO program development; highlight NEO program purposes/goals

_____ outline employee's responsibility in orientation process

_____ briefly review materials in "Welcome Package"; encourage later reading and follow-up questions

_____ explain mentoring concept; introduce mentor

_____ provide new employee an opportunity to ask questions

_____ Other (elaborate): _____

Comments:_____

III. ADDITIONAL MEETINGS/ACTIVITIES (first, second, third week, or as needed)

_____ coordinate special presentations as needed

_____ **initiate** periodic contact with mentor, new employee, and immediate supervisor following week one to check on progress, remind about maintaining checklists, etc. (note dates/types of contact, etc. on back of this sheet or in separate log)

_____ Other (elaborate):_____

IV. FOLLOW-UP ACTIVITIES

_____ frequently monitor mentor/new employee relationship, particularly during the first three weeks (note dates/types of contact, etc., on back of this sheet or in separate log)

_____ send NEO program evaluation I to new employee (at end of third or fourth week on job)

_____ send NEO program evaluation II to new employee (at end of three month orientation period)

_____ send NEO program evaluations to supervisor and NEO mentor (at end of three month NEO period)

_____ receive/file completed NEO program evaluation I from new employee

_____ receive/file completed NEO program evaluation II from new employee

_____ receive/file completed NEO program evaluation and checklist from immediate supervisor

_____ receive completed NEO program evaluation and checklist from NEO mentor

_____ write NEO Coordinator's evaluation summary based on others' input, e.g. formal evaluations/checklists; file for future program evaluation

_____ meet informally with all participants to debrief them and formally end the orientation process

_____ Other (elaborate):_____

an excellent job at orienting their new hires without benefit of a structured NEO program. However, it would be fool-hearty to assume that all supervisors are equally competent in this area. Good supervisors will recognize the value of a program designed to provide complete and consistent library-wide information to all new library employees.

Duties and responsibilities of immediate supervisors in a structured NEO approach might include:

- Overseeing the preparation of the new employee's work space before his or her first day on job (i.e., desk is clear and stocked with supplies);
- Introducing new employee to co-workers in immediate work area;
- Maintaining NEO checklist developed in conjunction with the NEO coordinator;
- Maintaining appropriate communication with the NEO coordinator regarding orientation progress, problems, etc.;
- Explaining to the new employee major library policies closely related to job performance (e.g.,lunch periods, breaks, scheduling, time sheets, "dress code," and calling in);
- Explaining unit/departmental-specific procedures;
- Coordinating routine orientation activities such as tour of immediate work area;
- Devoting special attention and time with the new employee to review the new employee's written job description, performance evaluation criteria and processes, etc.;
- Initiating periodic contact with the new employee to offer assistance, answer questions, see how things are going, etc.; and
- Participating in the NEO program evaluation.

> . . . it would be a fool-hearty assumption that all supervisors are equally competent in . . . orienting their new hires without benefit of a structured NEO program. Good supervisors will recognize the value of a program designed to provide complete and consistent library-wide information to all new library employees.

MENTORS

A fairly common practice in business and industry is to assign a veteran co-worker to each new employee for the purpose of serving as a resource person during the employee's initial settling-in period. Terminology in the literature varies as to what these co-workers are called—mentors, sponsors, and buddies are frequently

---

FIGURE 2-2 SUPERVISOR'S NEO CHECKLIST

New Employee:_____ Start Date:_____

Position:_____

Library Dept.:_____ Phone No.:_____

NEO Coordinator:_____ Phone/e-mail:_____

NEO Mentor:_____ Phone/e-mail:_____

GENERAL INSTRUCTIONS

Upon completion of each activity on the following checklist, record the date completed. Use N/A for any activity which does not apply to this particular orientation. An "Other" category has been included in each section of the checklist so that any activities unique to the new employee's position may be noted. Checklist items are not presented in any prioritized or imposed order.

I. ACTIVITIES PRIOR TO NEW EMPLOYEE'S STARTING DATE

_____ confirm new employee's starting date (verify with administrative office and NEO Coordinator)

_____ meet with NEO Coordinator; during meeting:

     _____ review NEO process and content; revise orientation checklists as needed

     _____ based on requirements of the position, determine possible need for special presentations

     _____ select and rank order mentor candidates

_____ prepare new employee's work space, e.g., stock supplies, get campus directory, etc.

_____ inform department/unit staff of new employee's arrival

_____ Other (elaborate):_____

Comments:_____

_____

II. INITIAL ACTIVITIES WITH THE NEW EMPLOYEE (NOTE: while the following checklist items/activities are listed as if the immediate supervisor actually conducts them, the supervisor may want to delegate some of the activities to the new employee's co-workers or mentor.)

_____ meet new employee upon his/her arrival at the library on their first day

_____ give new employee tour of immediate work area and introduce to co-workers

_____ review department/unit guidelines for the following:

     _____ breaks/break rooms   _____ pay periods/timesheets

     _____ lunch periods   _____ issuing of work keys

     _____ sick leave   _____ other:_____

--continued on back--

FIGURE 2-2 CONTINUED

_____ review job description with new employee; make sure employee has own copy

_____ review in detail the performance appraisal/pre-tenure evaluation procedures, timelines, etc.

_____ explain the new employee's position's role within the department or unit

_____ explain the role of the department/unit within the overall library structure

_____ explain the role of the library in relation to the parent organization

_____ allow breaks in providing information for new employee to read and digest information; try to avoid "information overload"

_____ provide new employee frequent opportunities to ask questions

_____ Other (elaborate):_____

Comments:_____

_____

III. ADDITIONAL ACTIVITIES (first, second, third week, or as needed)

_____ **initiate** periodic contact/discussion with new employee regarding their "settling in" (note date and type of contact):_____

_____ Other (elaborate):_____

Comments:_____

_____

IV. FOLLOW-UP ACTIVITIES

_____ meet with the new employee at the end of his/her probationary period to discuss NEO program effectiveness

_____ complete formal evaluation of NEO process and forward to NEO Coordinator along with this completed checklist

_____ Other (elaborate):_____

Comments:_____

_____

This completed checklist is to be returned to the NEO Coordinator at the end of the orientation period.

cited. At ISU, the term NEO mentor was adopted. Among all the aspects of the ISU NEO program, the mentoring component has been the most popular and most appreciated by new employees who have evaluated the program.

The NEO mentor is an experienced *peer-level* staff member who volunteers to be paired with a new employee to serve as a resource person for the new employee during the new employee's orientation period. To facilitate the new employee's interaction with staff members from other library divisions and units the mentor, if possible, should be from a division other than the new staff member's. Primary duties and responsibilities of the NEO Mentor might include:

- Maintaining the NEO Mentor checklist developed by the NEO coordinator and supervisor; conducting orientation activities as outlined on checklist within the specified time period (e.g., library tour and campus tour);
- Maintaining record of assistance offered to/requested by the new employee;
- Initiating frequent contact with the new employee, particularly during the first month, to see how things are going;
- Emphasizing to the new employee, from a peer perspective important Library policies, procedures, projects, etc.;
- Encouraging new employee interaction with other staff during breaks and lunches and through special programs, involvement in appropriate organizations, committees, etc.;
- In all NEO activities, striving to maintain objectivity in light of any personal biases regarding university/library policies, department/unit activities, individual personalities, etc.;
- Maintaining appropriate communication with the new employee's immediate supervisor and the NEO coordinator regarding progress, problems, observations, etc.; and
- Participating in the NEO program evaluation.

Selection of a mentor for a new employee should be done by the NEO coordinator and the new employee's immediate supervisor. Taking into consideration the new employee's job classification and responsibilities, the coordinator and supervisor should identify possible mentor candidates and rank them in terms of first choice, second choice, etc. When generating the list of mentor candidates, the NEO coordinator and immediate supervisor should

> The NEO Mentor is an experienced peer level staff member who volunteers to be paired with a new employee to serve as a resource person for the new employee during the new employee's orientation period.

try to reach agreement about the relative importance of such factors as age, gender, and general personality in their selections. ISU's experience in matching mentors and new employees has been that mentor/employee matches of the same gender and general age work best. Outgoing personality types almost always make better mentors than more passive, introverted staff members. Finally, mentor candidates need not be only those staff members who have been in their jobs for several years. Recent hires who have been on the job beyond the first three months are often very enthusiastic about serving as an NEO mentor. While they may not have the same level of detailed knowledge about the library and the larger institution, there is something to be said for the empathy they are able to provide a new employee having just gone through the settling-in process themselves.

Prior to approaching the first-choice mentor candidate to solicit his or her involvement, the NEO coordinator should contact the candidate's immediate supervisor to verify that the individual's participation in the NEO program would not interfere with his or her routine duties or the workflow or coverage of the office. While most supervisors will unhesitatingly approve one of their staff member's involvement in the NEO program as a new employee mentor, approval is not always a foregone conclusion since there may be major projects or deadlines in the unit that would be adversely affected by a staff member taking on an outside assignment. If supervisory approval is not possible for the first mentor candidate, the NEO coordinator should approach the second choice's supervisor. Once supervisory approval is obtained for a mentor, the NEO coordinator should approach the mentor candidate to see if they are interested in the assignment. For individuals who have never served as a mentor before or who have not attended a mentor training workshop (see Chapter 4), the coordinator should be prepared to discuss the overall NEO process and the mentor's role in it. The coordinator should also provide the mentor with a list of NEO program goals and duties of the NEO mentor.

INVOLVING OTHERS IN THE PROGRAM

Depending on the duties and responsibilities of a new employee, it may be necessary to call on certain individuals to share specialized information or provide unique demonstrations for the new

---

FIGURE 2-3 NEO MENTOR'S CHECKLIST

New Employee:_____ Start Date:_____

Position:_____

Library Dept.:_____ Phone No.:_____

NEO Coordinator:_____ Phone/e-mail:_____

Immed. Supervisor:_____ Phone/e-mail:_____

GENERAL INSTRUCTIONS

Upon completion of each activity on the following checklist, record the date completed. Use N/A for any activity which does not apply to this particular orientation. An "Other" category has been included in each section of the checklist so that any activities unique to the new employee's position may be noted. Checklist items are not presented in any prioritized or imposed order.

Special Note-- While serving as a mentor, please keep an informal record of the kinds of assistance offered to or requested by the new employee; also include the date of assistance in this record. This information will be particularly helpful in improving future orientations.

I. ACTIVITIES PRIOR TO NEW EMPLOYEE'S STARTING DATE

_____ meet with NEO Coordinator and/or new employee's immediate supervisor; discuss/clarify mentor's role as necessary

_____ if available, review resume/background information on new employee

_____ confirm new employee's starting date with NEO Coordinator and/or new employee's supervisor

_____ Other (elaborate):_____

Comments:_____

II. INITIAL ACTIVITIES WITH THE NEW EMPLOYEE (preferably first day on the job)

_____ introduction to new employee

_____ explain to the new employee your role as their mentor

_____ review "availability" for future contact, as appropriate, e.g. any irregularities in your working hours, give your phone extension, e-mail address and, if deemed appropriate, home phone number, physically locate your office for the employee, etc.

_____ actively encourage new employee to contact you as needed

_____ conduct any specific activities assigned by NEO Coordinator and new employee's supervisor, e.g., building tour

_____ break/lunch with new employee

_____ Other (elaborate):_____

Comments:_____

--continued on back--

FIGURE 2-3 CONTINUED

III. ADDITIONAL ACTIVITIES (first, second, third week, or as needed)

_____ arrange for an orientation to appropriate library organizations/committees; accompany new employee to such meetings and introduce him/her to the group prior to the beginning of business

_____ **initiate** contact with new employee just to see how they are doing (if possible, at least once a day during the first week)

_____ maintain appropriate communications with new employee's supervisor and the NEO Coordinator to keep them informed of NEO progression

_____ Other (elaborate):_____

Comments:_____

IV. FOLLOW-UP ACTIVITIES

_____ continue to initiate periodic contact with new employee

_____ maintain appropriate communication with NEO Coordinator and new employee's supervisor

_____ meet with new employee to end the formal mentoring relationship (time frame to be collectively determined by the mentor, immediate supervisor, and the NEO Coordinator)

_____ complete formal evaluation of NEO mentoring experience and forward to NEO Coordinator along with this completed checklist

_____ Other (elaborate):_____

Comments:_____

RECORD OF CONTACT AND ASSISTANCE OFFERED TO/REQUESTED BY NEW EMPLOYEE
(include date and brief explanation of assistance/type of contact; attach additional sheets as necessary):

_____   _____
Date   Contact
            _____

_____   _____
Date   Contact
            _____

_____   _____
Date   Contact
            _____

_____   _____
Date   Contact
            _____

This completed checklist is to be returned to the NEO Coordinator at the end of the orientation period.

employee. For example, it may be appropriate during an employee's first week or so to have an administrative office staff member provide a basic orientation to staff photocopying services; the instruction librarian might be scheduled to provide a basic introduction to the library's automated systems; or the chairs of various library committees and organizations might be asked to orient the new employee to in-house organizations and library governance. The need for and timing of any special presentations during any given orientation should be determined by the NEO coordinator, the new employee's supervisor, and the NEO mentor.

3 ANTICIPATING AND HANDLING PROBLEMS

No matter how much advance planning has taken place, there is no such thing as a perfect program. However, one of the distinguishing marks of a good program is that it includes a contingency planning component in its development. Contingency planning is a management technique that identifies alternative courses of action in the event that specific problems or threats are encountered during a program or process (Finch, *Encyclopedia of Management Techniques,* 35, 1985). In developing an NEO program, some attention must be given to the fact that things can and occasionally will go wrong. Some problems may be avoidable while others will not be; some can be anticipated, others not. Regardless, anticipation of the most likely problems is key. The program planners and the NEO coordinator should expect glitches in the NEO process and be prepared in advance to handle them. In preparing the initial program document, contingency plans of action should be spelled out in as detailed a manner as possible. As the program evolves and unanticipated problems come up, appropriate actions should be taken, documented, and their outcomes evaluated. Successes should be incorporated into the appropriate procedural sections of program documentation. Likewise, unsuccessful approaches to problem-solving and troubleshooting should be noted so that all who consult the program document have a complete history of the program's evolution. As the old saying goes, "Those who cannot remember the past are condemned to repeat it."

Among the more predictable problems that might arise in a new employee orientation program are periods of high staff turnover that will tax the time of those involved in orienting new replacements; ineffective participants; short notice of a new employee's arrival; dropouts; staff resistance to the program; mismatched mentors and new employees; and a distorted impression of the NEO coordinator's role. Practical suggestions for dealing with each of these situations follow.

> The program planners and the NEO coordinator should expect glitches in the NEO process and be prepared in advance to handle them.

PERIODS OF HIGH TURNOVER

In Chapter 1, in discussing how to assess the existing organizational structure of the library, one of the questions recommended for consideration in the process was: What is the average annual turnover among library staff? This number should be fairly easy to determine by contacting the library administrative office or the organization's central personnel office. An average number of all library turnovers broken down by position classification (professional and support staff) should be calculated from the annual figures of the last three to five years. This number will give program planners and the NEO coordinator a general idea of the number of NEO participants that can be expected in an average year. However, averages do fluctuate, and upward extremes in this area can cause problems if they are not anticipated and planned for.

At ISU, during the NEO program planning phase, the average annual staff turnover was calculated at approximately four, almost all of which were support staff positions. Turnover among professional staff averaged less than one per year. During the first year of the program's pilot implementation, the actual number of NEO participants was about the expected average, the next year it was lower, but the third year it was considerably higher among the support staff ranks.

The pace of NEO activities can become rather hectic when several new employees are in the orientation process at any given point in time. The best defense against this problem is to have a supply of all NEO documentation and support materials on hand before they are actually needed. Unassigned NEO documentation files, containing participants' checklists, the core content of the welcome packet, and the glossary of library terms (the latter two items are discussed in Chapter 5), can be preassembled so that once notification is received that a new employee will be starting on a particular date, all that is needed to activate the documentation file for that new employee is a folder label with his or her name on it. Since core content is already gathered, all that is then needed is a bit of tailoring by adding to the file any other materials unique to the new hire's particular job responsibilities. Just as you should have preassembled documentation folders ready in advance, you should have one or more versions of a standardized welcome letter (*see* Chapter 4) in an electronic file so that it only needs to be personalized before being sent to the new employee.

Another way of addressing high turnover is for the NEO coordinator to clarify any orientation activities that might be combined for two new employees who started the job at about the same time. Even though a one-on-one approach was presented as the ideal approach earlier, it is simply not always possible. And as noted in Chapter 1 in the discussion of program structure, depending on overall library size and annual turnover, a group approach to certain activities may be the only way to go. Depending on the nature of a particular orientation activity, switching to a one-on-*two* or one-on-*three* approach probably would not compromise the personal interaction factor significantly, particularly if the individuals planning and conducting the activity are reminded to keep the session as informal and personalized as possible. In fact, combining some activities for two or more new employees might actually facilitate their interpersonal interaction with each other and with other staff.

INEFFECTIVE PARTICIPANTS

In the earliest stages of implementing a new employee orientation program, everyone, even the NEO coordinator, is new to the process. Some patience and flexibility will have to be shown by all participants as everyone learns his or her roles. Over time, through direct observation and information gathered as a part of the program's ongoing evaluation, the NEO coordinator will be able to identify those individuals who function well in the program and those who, for whatever reason, seem to be consistently unable to carry out their NEO responsibilities effectively or on time. One of the most likely reasons for this problem may be that an individual has more than he or she can do during the average workday—despite his or her willingness to participate, the person may not be able to find or make the time required for mentoring or engaging in other activities involved in the orientation program. If and when this problem becomes apparent, the NEO coordinator should discreetly step in by increasing personal contact with the individual (most likely a mentor, but occasionally a supervisor) to check on progress, make suggestions, offer assistance, and provide informal pep talks. The NEO coordinator should avoid over-reacting to an overworked mentor or supervisor. More harm than good would come from making an issue of the situation, since making it an issue would most likely have a very damaging effect (and worse, affect) on the new employee if he or she found out; the new employee might feel responsible for the problem.

Once a particular orientation has ended wherein the mentor did not function very well, the NEO coordinator should make note so that the past problem can be taken into careful consideration before involving the same individual in any future orientations. If the same individual happens to volunteer for mentoring in the

More harm than good would come from making an issue of [an ineffective mentor or supervisor], since making it an issue would most likely have a very damaging effect (and worse, affect) on the new employee if he or she found out; the new employee might feel responsible for the problem.

future, the NEO coordinator should discuss the earlier problem, acknowledging that the individual was probably just very busy at the time. The coordinator should then ask the volunteer if he or she would now have the time to devote to the upcoming mentoring duties. Depending on the individual's response, the NEO coordinator will have to make a judgment call. Regardless of whether the individual is used in future orientations, the fact that a problem came up at all indicates that increased emphasis may be needed in the mentor training workshops (see Chapter 4) about the time commitment required of staff members who want to serve as NEO mentors.

In the case of a supervisor who has had problems with his or her responsibilities in the orientation process, the NEO coordinator will need to spend some time talking openly about the problem with the individual. Obviously, the supervisor's role in the orientation process is not an optional activity. The NEO coordinator should offer to go over any aspects of the program that are not clear to the supervisor. The coordinator should also give the supervisor an opportunity to offer suggestions about how he or she thinks the situation could be improved. The coordinator could also suggest that the supervisor delegate certain activities on the supervisor's NEO checklist to other department or unit staff. Hopefully this will solve or at least improve future situations. If not, the problem should be addressed at a higher administrative level as a matter of the supervisor's job performance.

It is not beyond the realm of possibility that a new employee turns out to have problems functioning in NEO activities and/or relationships. Sometimes employees with poor interpersonal skills or serious personal problems do make it through the interviewing and hiring process. Depending on how the problem is initially identified, the NEO coordinator should first investigate the situation to rule out a mismatch between the new employee and his or her mentor or some other fairly obvious cause. The new employee's supervisor should be informed by the coordinator that there may be a problem and should be consulted in case the supervisor has any information or insights that might help resolve the situation. If the coordinator and immediate supervisor ultimately decide that the problem is with the new employee and not the NEO program, the mentor, or whoever, or whatever, the immediate supervisor should intervene and take the lead in dealing with whatever the problem is. Depending on the nature of the problem (e.g., attitude, personality, or personal problems), the NEO coordinator should be supportive of the new employee by reminding the immediate supervisor about any employee assistance program options that might be available and appropriate in the situation. Regarding continuation of the NEO process under these circumstances, the coordinator may want to recommend to the mentor that he or she minimize or suspend contact with the new employee until further notice. The NEO coordinator should maintain contact with the new employee, but only in close communication with the immediate supervisor. In the event that such a situation arises, the mentor, coordinator, and immediate supervisor should be mindful of the need for strict confidentiality.

Last, but certainly not least among the NEO participants, if the NEO coordinator is not functioning effectively, other participants will likely notice this at some point in the process. In such cases, hopefully those noticing the problem will call it to the attention of library administration. Otherwise, the problem will go unchecked until it is identified during the written evaluation phase of the program (discussed in Chapters 7 through 9). Obviously, of all the participants in the process, an ineffective NEO coordinator could have the most negative impact on the overall program since, in effect, it would lack adequate overall coordination and would be unfocused and disorganized. However, if library administration is truly devoted to the NEO concept and supportive of the program, the problem will be noticed and dealt with from the top.

SHORT NOTICE

Depending on channels of communication, it is not always possible to get a lot of advance notice about when a new employee is actually going to begin the job. The NEO coordinator should be aware of open positions within the library, the current status of search and interview schedules, and when employment offers have been formalized. The ease with which the coordinator can get into the various communication queues to stay abreast of such information obviously depends on the local situation. However, depending on the positions that are vacant, the NEO coordinator and supervisor of the future new employee could begin preliminary discussions and make certain program decisions even before anyone is hired. For example, any special orientation activities or special materials or information beyond what's included in the core content of the welcome packet could be identified based on the requirements of the vacant position; and possible mentor candidates could be identified in terms of assigned division and classification.

Under ideal circumstances, a welcome letter is sent to a new employee about a week before he or she starts the job (see Chapter 4) to generally welcome the person to the library and let him or her know about the NEO program. In the case of short notice, if there is not enough time to get a welcome letter out, the NEO coordinator might want to call the individual at home to let the person know that he or she is expected and that a special program is in place to help the individual get settled in. If a letter or call is not possible, the NEO coordinator should try to make informal contact with the new employee as soon after his or her arrival as possible to let the employee know that there is a structured orientation process and that it will begin as soon as possible. The NEO coordinator should then do whatever necessary to get the process started. If NEO documentation files are made up in advance, as recommended in the discussion of high turnover, dealing with the problem of short notice is simplified.

DROPOUTS

The NEO process is subject to participants dropping out temporarily (due to an unexpected leave of absence or extended illness) or permanently (due to taking another job). Obviously, if the new employee drops out of the process permanently, there is really no problem, perhaps only the unfortunate regret of the lost time and energy invested up to that point.

If the original NEO mentor leaves the program, the NEO coordinator should be able to call on another staff member who already has mentoring experience. An experienced mentor should be able to slide into the vacant spot without any problem. If an experienced mentor replacement is not available, the NEO coordinator can call on someone who has attended a mentor training workshop but has not yet actually served as a mentor. He or she will probably be eager finally to get into the program. Also, the use of a mentor's checklist as presented in Chapter 2 will make it much easier for a replacement mentor to move in and quickly determine what has been done already and what still needs to be done. Having to replace a mentor at any point in the NEO process does not allow much time to take into consideration the desirability of matching the new employee and mentor by age, gender, and personality factors as discussed in the previous chapter; however, this may be unavoidable.

If a new employee's supervisor has to drop out of the program for an extended period of time, it is the library administration's responsibility to appoint someone (usually within the same unit or department) to serve in a temporary or acting supervisory capacity for the unit. If the acting supervisor is expected to assume all regular supervisory responsibilities, then involvement in the NEO program would be included. As already pointed out in the case of a mentor who might have to drop out, the supervisor's NEO checklist will help the acting supervisor pick up where his or her predecessor left off. To lessen the strain that is likely to be felt by the individual thrown into an acting supervisory role, the NEO coordinator should be prepared to take up any slack in the NEO activities generally assigned to the new employee's immediate supervisor.

The loss of the NEO coordinator in the middle of the orientation process can have a more negative impact on the NEO process than losing a mentor or supervisor since the coordinator is responsible for seeing that everything gets done by the right participants at the right time. Like any other position in any other organization, there should be a general system or procedure of back up for the coordinator. A detailed program document outlining the entire NEO process and the specific duties of the NEO coordinator and other participants will make it much easier for a replacement coordinator to assume the role at the last minute. And as noted above, the use of checklists, in this case the coordinator's NEO checklist, will allow the back up coordinator to move the process along without a major break in continuity. After the initial program document is developed, the NEO coordinator must make sure that it is updated as the program evolves. Another way to have a backup coordinator in place is to have the original coordinator occasionally involve a colleague in the coordinating aspects of the program just in case a backup is ever needed.

SCATTERED STAFF RESISTANCE TO THE PROGRAM

There is probably no staff of any size in any type of organization that does not have one or more malcontents and/or general resistors to any kind of change. If there is staff resistance to implementing an NEO program, the NEO coordinator and/or library administration should try to determine the specific reason or reasons for the resistance. Like anywhere else, at ISU, staff resistance to certain types of changes (e.g., the implementation of a new program or service) sometimes is merely a function of "anti-administration" personalities; the resistance is not based on what is considered good for the organization, but rather on what the resistor does or does not want to do. Usually, the reputations and dispositions of these types of staff members precede them, and as a result, their resistance to innovation is usually of no major consequence, just mildly irritating. If legitimate reasons cannot be provided or discovered, or if recalcitrants cannot be converted to a more supportive point of view, probably the best advice is simply not to involve these individuals in the program.

Where staff resistance becomes more of a problem is when it comes from a resistant supervisor. It has already been acknowledged that some supervisors may feel threatened by a perceived outsider (a.k.a., the NEO coordinator) taking over the orientation of their new employees, or perhaps some supervisors might interpret the implementation of an NEO program as an inference that they have not been doing their jobs well. In this case, the NEO coordinator should discuss the problem frankly with the supervisors to alleviate any feelings of resentment, trying to clarify the purposes of the NEO program and the supporting role of the NEO coordinator. Beyond this, all the NEO coordinator can do is to try to let actions speak louder than words, (i.e., when working with a reluctant supervisor during an actual orientation, the coordinator can make the experience so supportive and enjoyable that the supervisor will welcome future opportunities for involvement). If this tact is unsuccessful, the NEO coordinator must make a judgment call on whether to refer the problem to library administration. As already noted in the earlier discussion of how to handle an ineffective (as opposed to resistant) supervisor in the NEO process, a supervisor's participation in the NEO program is not optional but rather is a necessary responsibility of a supervisor. It is the administration's responsibility to communicate this to supervisors and address any continuing problems as issues in supervisors' job performance evaluations.

MISMATCHED MENTORS AND NEW EMPLOYEES

Despite whatever care is taken by the NEO coordinator and the new employee's supervisor to make a compatible match between a NEO mentor and an employee, mismatches can happen—sometimes personalities just clash. Hopefully, such an occurrence will be exceedingly rare or, better yet, nonexistent. However, if it does happen, the most important thing for the NEO coordinator to do is to intervene quickly and diplomatically. Intervention is much easier if the NEO coordinator has already set the stage by openly acknowledging the possibility that a mentor and new employee may simply turn out not to get along.

When the NEO coordinator first meets with the mentor prior to the new employee's starting date, discussion of the mentor's role should include specific mention, and emphasis on the fact that the mentor and employee are not bound to the relationship if it does not work out. This should also be communicated and emphasized to prospective mentors in the mentor training workshops (*see* Chapter 4). The mentor should be instructed to notify the NEO coordinator at the first indication that there might be a problem. The NEO coordinator should offer assurance to the mentor that if this situation does arise, the coordinator will investigate immediately and confidentially. In addition to discussing the possibility of a mismatch with the mentor, the coordinator should let the new employee know during their initial meeting how to handle the situation in the unlikely event it should arise.

If, at any time during the new orientation period, the mentor, new employee, or supervisor reports or even mildly suggests that there appears to be an interpersonal problem between the new employee and the mentor, the NEO coordinator should assign high priority to finding out what is going on. Regardless of the situation, the coordinator must first make a judgment as to whether the perceived problem is due to some simple misunderstanding or a glitch in communications between the two. If the NEO coordinator determines that this is the case, the problem might be resolved easily just by sitting down and talking. All reasonable attempts should be made to salvage the relationship. It is not inconceivable that a personality clash (or whatever the problem) may be so obvious or severe that the coordinator's decision to attempt salvaging the relationship will be an easy one. If it becomes necessary to replace the original mentor, a replacement should be made as soon as possible. Should this happen well into the orientation period, say after a month or two, the NEO coordinator may be able to take over any remaining mentoring responsibilities.

In the event of a mismatch between mentor and new employee, the NEO coordinator should not be concerned initially with who was to blame, if anyone. Sometimes problems arise as a result of unanticipated, unavoidable circumstances beyond anyone's control. However, in the interest of avoiding the problem in future orientations, at some point after the problem has been dealt with, the NEO coordinator should spend some time analyzing the situation to determine (if possible) what might have gone wrong. Could the problem have been avoided? Could it happen again? A mismatch might signal any one of several causes that the coordinator should note. Problems arising from a mismatch could mean that the individual serving as the mentor may not be suited to mentoring. Perhaps this individual should not be used as a mentor in the future. Or perhaps the problems stemming from the mismatch are an early indication that a new employee has a problem with interpersonal skills. Again, the NEO coordinator is put in a position where he or she has to make a judgment call as to what is at the root of the problem. Using his or her best judgment, the NEO coordinator should communicate conclusions to the appropriate supervisors. The extent to which such communication should be formal or informal will depend largely on the specific situation and the local administrative environment.

Over the past six years of ISU Libraries' NEO program, there has been only one instance in which a new employee and mentor had an interpersonal problem, and it was only after the new employee's evaluation of her orientation experience that any friction was reported. Prior to that time, nothing was noticed by the NEO coordinator or the new employee's supervisor (or by the mentor, based on her evaluation comments). At ISU, this problem has never occurred to the extent that it required dissolution of the mentor/new employee relationship. However, should it occur, the NEO coordinator should not overstate the case or dwell on the situation, particularly when discussing it with the new employee involved, since this could be very unsettling if the new employee is somewhat of an introverted worrier. New employees experience enough new job jitters without having them unintentionally compounded by an overly thorough coordinator.

GETTING CAUGHT IN THE MIDDLE

Speaking from personal experience, one of the most rewarding aspects of serving as an NEO coordinator is the close working relationships formed with many of the new employees who have gone through the ISU NEO program. Prior to the NEO program, I would have never had the opportunity to interact with some staff members whom I have come to know and respect well. Unfortunately, however, these rewards come with a potential price tag. While an NEO coordinator must be sincere in his or her nurturing and support of all new employees, sometimes a new employee might over-interpret the relationship to the extent that the coordinator all of a sudden finds himself or herself playing in-house counselor and personal adviser on issues that go beyond what is appropriate for a NEO coordinator/new employee relationship. In initial meetings with the new employee, the NEO coordinator should be clear in letting the new employee know that he or she is always there to answer questions, offer advice regarding the organization, and serve as a sounding board for new ideas. However, at some point in these interactions with the new employee (though probably not during their first meeting), the coordinator needs to openly acknowledge the awkward position in which he or she would be placed if the new employee is having problems with his or her supervisor and comes to the NEO coordinator for help. Aside from just letting them get the problem off their chest and perhaps organize their thoughts by talking about it with someone, the new employee should not expect the NEO coordinator to intervene on his or her behalf or offer any advice beyond being asked, "Have you talked with [whoever] about how you're feeling about [the problem/situation]?" If the employer's reply is "no," the employer should be told to expect the coordinator to reply along the lines of, "I understand how you must be feeling, but the only way to solve the problem is to address it with those who are directly involved." At ISU, the NEO coordinator's role is *not* administrative and, therefore, has no jurisdiction over personnel matters that involve the employee/supervisor relationship. The NEO coordinator should avoid getting caught in the middle of situations where loyalties and confidentiality are strained. The best way to do this is to realize that it can happen and address it with each new employee at some point during early orientation discussions.

THE IMPORTANCE OF A STAFF DEVELOPMENT COMMITTEE

At ISU, a Library Staff Development Committee was established back in 1989 as a standing committee. It replaced a subcommittee of the Library Faculty Assembly, the official governing/advisory body for professional librarians who hold academic faculty rank. The same library consultant who was mentioned in the Introduction of this manual, and who recommended the development and implementation of a new employee orientation program, also recommended that the existing library faculty committee be expanded in scope and charge. The original library faculty staff development committee did not address the continuing education/developmental needs of the library's support staff, nor was there an equivalent committee or group representing support staff. As is probably true in all academic libraries, ISU Libraries' support staff outnumbers professional staff by more than two to one. From the standpoint of day-to-day library operations, it almost goes without saying, particularly in today's automated library environment, that the job-related developmental needs of support staff are no less important than those of library professionals.

Appointed by the Dean of Library Services, the Library Staff Development Committee consists of five members, representing all divisions and levels of staff (one library faculty member from Public Services, one library faculty member from Technical Services, one at large faculty member, and two support staff members). Each committee member serves a two-year term; terms are staggered for continuity. Though not spelled out to this level of detail at ISU, from an NEO program standpoint, the committee should also include in its five-member composition at least one relatively new library staff member if possible. Inclusion of a new employee strengthens the committee's overall purview. Consideration might also be given to having the NEO coordinator serve as an *ex officio* member of the committee.

The committee advises library administration on the planning, coordination, and evaluation of the libraries' overall staff development program. As part of the program evaluation component of its charge, the committee serves as advisory group to the NEO coordinator and makes recommendations to strengthen the NEO program. The committeee also conducts surveys of library staff regarding perceived developmental needs and, in response, organizes and publicizes staff development programs of interest to staffers.

A library staff development committee can be an important group within the administrative structure of any type or size of library. Regarding an NEO program, a staff development committee could prove invaluable during initial development. Assuming that such a committee represents all levels and classifications of library staff, its members could take an active role in the development and field testing of NEO program materials. The committee could also serve as sounding board and advisor to the NEO coordinator, particularly in situations where the NEO coordinator has to make a judgment call about the performance of an NEO program participant (e.g., the ineffective supervisor or mentor). Finally, a library staff development committee would build in additional accountability for the NEO coordinator. If no such group exists in your library, serious consideration should be given to the creation of one, regardless of whether an NEO program is offered.

4 PRIOR TO THE NEW EMPLOYEE'S START DATE

During the initial implementation of an NEO program, individuals who ultimately will participate as mentors and supervisors will have questions about the program in general and about their individual roles in particular. Other staff members will likely be curious about the new program, too. If initial planning and development of the NEO program include input from various staff via surveys, brainstorming sessions, etc., as discussed in Chapter 1, the majority of staff will have a general idea about the NEO concept. However, as soon as an actual program is outlined based on the information gathered during program development, the particulars about the program should be shared with the entire library staff.

Providing an appropriate amount of background information about an NEO program can be handled in a variety of ways. A complete, detailed program document should be made available through the NEO coordinator's and/or library administrative office for review by anyone interested. A brief (one or two page) summary highlighting the major components of the NEO program could be drafted and distributed to all staff. A more formal route for clueing in existing staff about the NEO program is to present a structured workshop, complete with the distribution of selected documents (checklists, evaluations, etc.) and use of overhead transparencies. Multiple sessions should be offered at various times of the day to accommodate service coverage and varying staff schedules. A less formal method for updating staff on the program's development and implementation would be to hold a brown-bag lunch for interested employees at which the NEO coordinator informally discusses the program and answers questions that anyone might have. Regardless of *how* the staff is informed about the program, "Who does what, when, and why?" are all questions that should be addressed before the program is actually implemented.

At ISU, staff were most curious about the mentoring component of the NEO program. While many members expressed interest in participating as mentors in the NEO program, their eagerness was tempered with a discernible amount of apprehension about what exactly was involved and whether they were cap-

> Regardless of how the staff is informed of the program, "who does what, when and why?" is the question that should be addressed before the program is actually implemented.

able of mentoring. Without enough initial information, some were not sure that they should make the commitment to serve as a mentor. This apprehension was most noticeable among support staff.

MENTOR TRAINING WORKSHOPS

Since the NEO mentor is a major contributor to the overall tone and ultimate success of the program, potential mentors should be given special attention. A good way to clarify the mentoring role, recruit mentors for the program, and allay any staff apprehension about mentoring is to offer mentor training workshops. Anyone and everyone among the library staff should be encouraged to attend a mentor workshop. In promoting the workshops, it should be stressed that attending one does not constitute a commitment on the part of the staff member to serve as an NEO mentor. The NEO mentoring workshops should be conducted by the NEO coordinator.

Since new employees come and go from all ranks and classifications of the library staff, anyone is a potential mentor. Even supervisors might find themselves as mentors for newly hired peer-level colleagues in other library departments and units.

The primary purposes of the mentor workshop are to provide mentor volunteers with an overview of the entire NEO program and to define clearly the roles and responsibilities of mentors and the importance of mentoring within the program. Any staff member who is to serve as a mentor should have attended a workshop.

The following discussion of several key elements in the mentoring process is presented to serve as a general guide for identifying and organizing the content for mentor workshops.

Discuss the Purpose of the Mentor Training Workshops and Provide a Brief Overview of How the Workshop Is Organized: Learners can usually focus their attentions to an instructional situation sooner when they have a general idea from the outset as to what is going to be covered in the workshop or seminar.

The workshop instructor should devote the first five to ten minutes to an overview of the workshop, including the workshop's goals and objectives. Since the NEO coordinator will be interested in evaluating the ultimate effectiveness of the workshop, participants need to know what it set out to do in order to evaluate

> The primary purposes of the mentor workshop are to provide mentor volunteers with an overview of the entire NEO program and to define clearly the roles and responsibilities of mentors and the importance of mentoring within the program.

it and, thereby, assist the coordinator in determining whether or not the goals and objectives of the workshop were met. Depending on how formal the workshop leader wants to get, a handout or transparency could be developed that includes a formal goal statement followed by specific objectives for the workshop. A transparency containing goals and objectives in key-word form and/or a more detailed handout could serve as a visual and mental focal point as each is being discussed.

As noted above, some workshop participants will come to the workshop with questions already in mind about what the NEO program and mentoring are all about. So, to get these individuals' minds off their questions (when to ask them, how to phrase them in front of the group, etc.) and lessen the likelihood of their interrupting the workshop leader in their eagerness to get their questions answered, it is wise to let them know up front the kinds of things that will be emphasized in the workshop. Perhaps an outline of the information to be covered, and the order in which it will be presented, would be appropriate. Sometimes individuals need the reassurance of knowing that they can keep up with what is being presented by mentally (or actually) checking each item on the outline as it is covered. Further, regardless of how interesting the workshop is, the clockwatchers in such groups, and there are always several, will appreciate a printed contents outline. Since a content outline can serve as a gauge of how much longer the workshop is likely to last, the clockwatchers can focus on the contents rather than what time it is.

In wrapping up the introductory portion of the workshop, the instructor should encourage the group to ask questions and offer any insights that might occur to them during the course of the workshop. In light of the subsequent evaluation of the workshop, the instructor should note (either mentally or, better, in writing) especially perceptive comments, reactions, or questions from workshop participants. These insights can only serve to make future workshops and the overall NEO program better.

Present an Overview of the Total NEO Program Process: In order for workshop participants to understand the role of the NEO mentor, it is essential that they have a general understanding of the overall NEO program. Care should be taken here not to dwell too long on the overall program; rather, the workshop instructor should cover the program's general organization, then quickly zero in on the specific roles and responsibilities of the mentor and his or her interrelationships with other program participants, i.e., the

... the instructor should encourage the group to ask questions and offer any insights that might occur to them during the course of the workshop.

new employee, the NEO coordinator, and the new employee's immediate supervisor. One way of presenting an overview of the NEO program is to develop one or more simple drawings diagraming of the major participants and their interrelationships in the program. The diagrams could be presented in an overhead projection and/or a handout. The sample transparency masters here can be used as a focal point for starting the discussion about the various players in the NEO process. Given the importance of communications among all participants, it is visually emphasized in the first transparency example. The second transparency could follow the first, allowing the workshop instructor to zero in on the interactions between the NEO coordinator and the NEO mentor. Another way of summarizing the program without going into a time-consuming discussion of program details during the mentor training workshop is to develop a one-page narrative summary that highlights all aspects of the NEO process (see example provided). Reduced versions of major transparency masters could be included on the back of the summary. Attendees could then review and consider the summary and the visuals after the workshop, and refer to the handout as needed in the future.

Detailed Discussion of the Duties and Responsibilities of NEO Mentors: A fairly detailed listing of recommended duties and responsibilities for all major NEO participants was presented in Chapter 2. During the mentor training workshop, the workshop instructor should spend considerable time going over each of these responsibilities. Whenever possible, even though it may seem obvious, a clear rationale should be presented for why a particular duty has been assigned to the mentor. Also whenever possible, real and hypothetical situations should be used to illustrate a particular responsibility and reinforce its relevance to the overall NEO process.

A question that can definitely be anticipated by the instructor that will be on the minds of most of those in attendance has to do with the time requirement/commitment necessary to serve as a mentor. In today's automated library, despite the fact that many outside our profession might assume that computers and electronic systems have made our jobs easier, most staff members already feel overwhelmed, if not overworked. Why *volunteer* for any additional responsibilities? On the other hand, ISU's experience has shown that the best mentors are those individuals who welcome the change of pace afforded by the role of mentor. Most find the interpersonal-interaction aspects of the role very rewarding and welcome the change in the routine. The best mentors also seem

FIGURE 4-1 SAMPLE TRANSPARENCY MASTER: 1 of 5

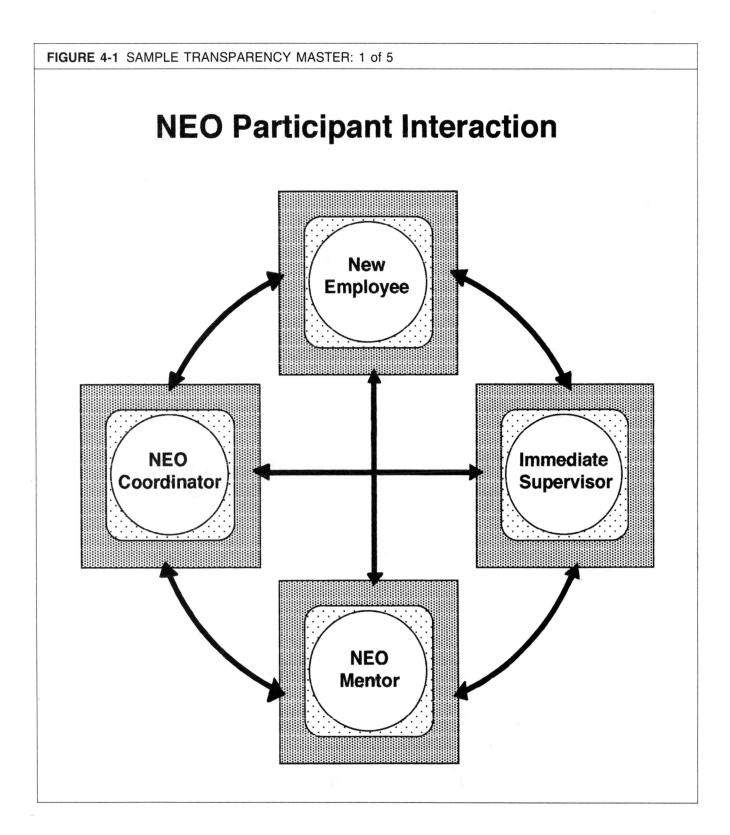

NEO Participant Interaction

FIGURE 4-1 SAMPLE TRANSPARENCY MASTER: 2 of 5

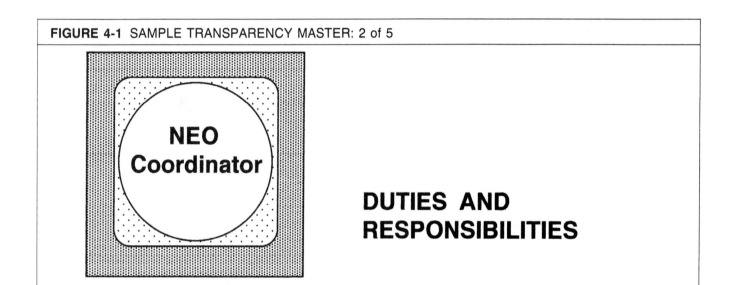

NEO Coordinator

DUTIES AND RESPONSIBILITIES

* trains/coaches NEO Mentors

* coordinates all pre-start date arrangements

* in cooperation with Immediate Supervisor, determines NEO content and selects Mentor

* meets with new employee to introduce NEO Program

* maintains contact with all participants throughout 3-month orientation period

* oversees NEO Program evaluation procedures

* modifies NEO Program as appropriate

FIGURE 4-1 SAMPLE TRANSPARENCY MASTER: 3 of 5

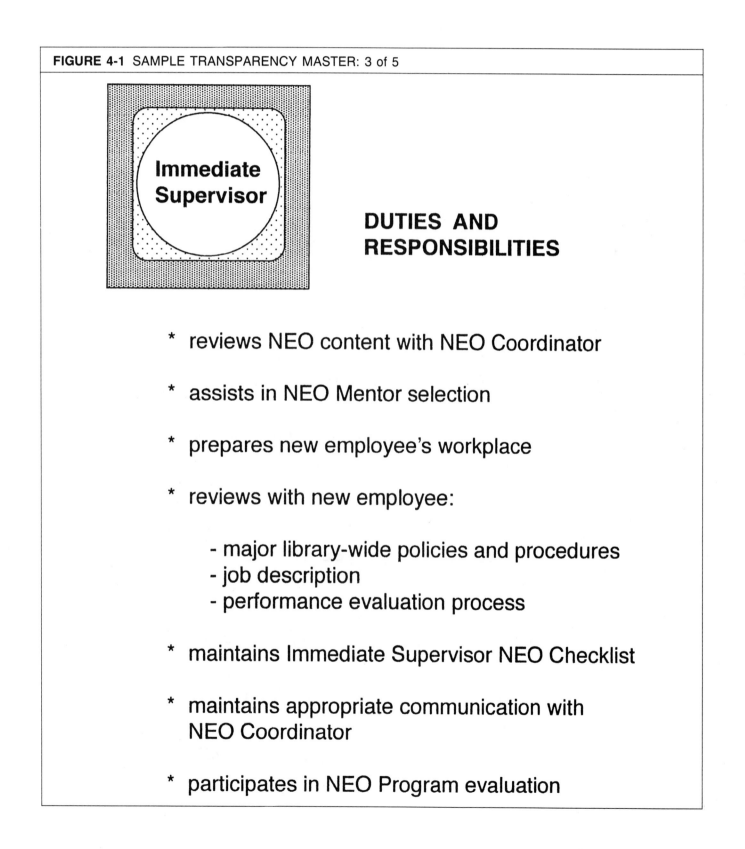

Immediate Supervisor

DUTIES AND RESPONSIBILITIES

* reviews NEO content with NEO Coordinator

* assists in NEO Mentor selection

* prepares new employee's workplace

* reviews with new employee:

    - major library-wide policies and procedures
    - job description
    - performance evaluation process

* maintains Immediate Supervisor NEO Checklist

* maintains appropriate communication with NEO Coordinator

* participates in NEO Program evaluation

FIGURE 4-1 SAMPLE TRANSPARENCY MASTER: 4 of 5

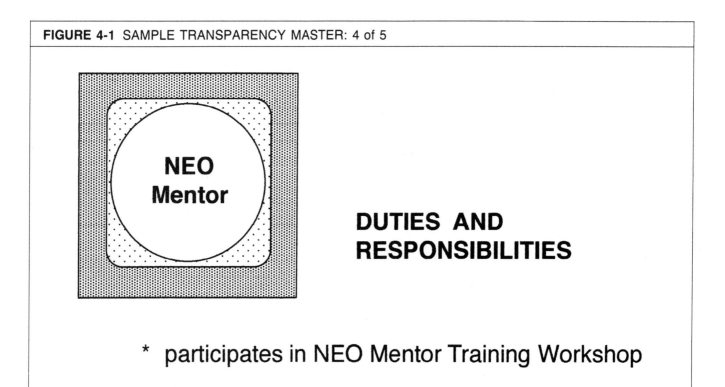

NEO Mentor

DUTIES AND RESPONSIBILITIES

* participates in NEO Mentor Training Workshop

* reviews NEO Content with NEO Coordinator

* reviews major Library policies and procedures

* facilitates new employee interaction with other staff

* initiates frequent contact with new employee

* maintains NEO Mentor checklist

* participates in NEO Program evaluation

FIGURE 4-1 SAMPLE TRANSPARENCY MASTER: 5 of 5

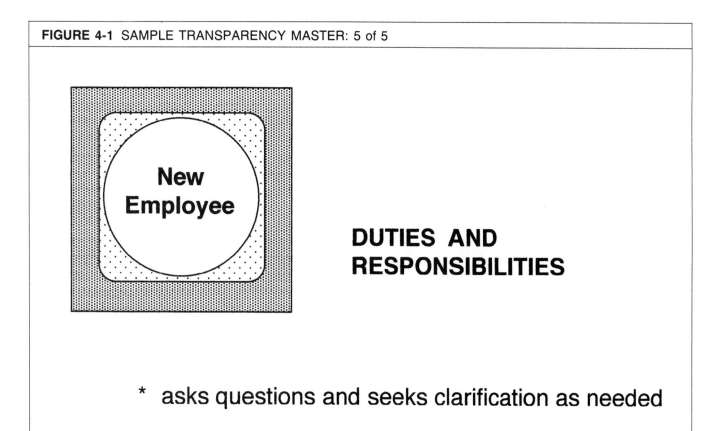

New Employee

DUTIES AND RESPONSIBILITIES

* asks questions and seeks clarification as needed

* reviews NEO Program materials

* interacts with NEO Mentor, Immediate Supervisor and NEO Coordinator

* participates in NEO scheduled activities

* participates in NEO Program evaluation

FIGURE 4-1 PROGRAM SUMMARY EXAMPLE

An Overview of
Indiana State University Libraries' NEO Program

The NEO program for ISU Libraries involves individualized orientation activities conducted during a new employee's first few days on the job, and continuing, as needed, throughout the initial months of his/her employment. The NEO program is designed for new full-time employees of ISU Libraries--faculty, biweekly staff, and administrators. The program can also be adapted for new temporary and part-time employees, depending on the terms of appointment. The program does not provide for student assistants since an orientation program is already in place for them. The NEO program is administered by the Department of Library Instruction & Orientation (LI&O). The LI&O department head serves as coordinator of the NEO program.

Prior to a new employee's starting date, the NEO coordinator and the new employee's Immediate Supervisor meet to determine appropriate orientation content for the particular position. They also discuss candidates for NEO Mentor. The NEO Coordinator meets with the supervisor of the mentor candidate to make sure that the supervisor approves of the mentor selection. A "Welcome Letter" to the new employee is sent by the NEO coordinator, generally informing him/her about the orientation program. The NEO Coordinator also assembles a "Welcome Packet" to give the new employee during their first meeting. The "Welcome Packet" includes basic library information, e.g. library brochure, staff phone list, organizational chart and department descriptions, library staff handbook, glossary of library terms and abbreviations, etc.

The orientation period for a new Library employee is three months. Ideally, the majority of NEO program activities take place during the new employee's first few weeks of employment. These activities are semi-structured in that they require scheduling of one or more orientation sessions; each session is flexible in terms of duration, content covered, and order of presentation. During the session(s) the NEO Coordinator: discusses the rationale and goals of the NEO program, provides an overview of the what the NEO program includes, reviews materials in the "Welcome Package," explains the libraries' organizational structure, discusses the NEO mentoring process, and introduces the new employee to his/her Mentor. The new employee and Mentor have considerable flexibility in determining when and why they will get together. Their activities might include a facilities tour, introductions to staff in departments other than the new employee's, and general discussion of internal policies and procedures, e.g. photocopying, staff organizations, sick leave, etc. Throughout the orientation process, the NEO Coordinator, NEO Mentor, and Immediate Supervisor maintain checklists of information covered and activities completed.

Following the first week of orientation, activities become less structured. The Immediate Supervisor and NEO Mentor should make frequent contact with the new employee to check on his/her settling in, and also respond to questions/contacts initiated by the new employee. After three or four weeks, the NEO Coordinator should meet with the new employee to discuss his/her orientation experience. The new employee is given the first of two program evaluation instruments to complete and return to the Coordinator within a couple of days. Throughout the orientation period, the NEO Coordinator records all input from the new employee, Immediate Supervisor, and NEO Mentor for later use in program review and evaluation.

The remainder of the orientation period is very informal. The Supervisor, Mentor, and NEO Coordinator continue to initiate periodic contact with the new employee, maintaining records of types of contact and assistance offered to/requested by the new employee. The orientation period ends after the new employee's first three months on the job. At that time, the NEO Coordinator distributes evaluation instruments to all participants, requesting that they critically evaluate the program based on their participation. They are also asked to return their completed checklist. Upon receipt of all evaluation materials and participant checklists, the NEO Coordinator reviews and files them for future use in overall program evaluation.

to exhibit considerable pride in the fact that they are playing an active role in helping a co-worker adjust to the workplace.

At least during the initial implementation of an NEO program, it will be difficult for the workshop instructor to be any more specific about the time requirement than to say that it will depend on numerous factors, all related to what knowledge and experience a new employee brings to his or her work environment. Assuming that ISU mentors' experiences are transferable to libraries of other types and sizes, the amount of time will vary between one to two hours per week. What the mentor is likely to find is that much of the contact is quick and informal, e.g., a brief telephone call to see how the new employee is doing, a quick personal note, or a short E-mail message. The biggest blocks of time that a mentor will likely spend with a new employee will be during the first week or two of their relationship. A first meeting for introductions, general conversation, and perhaps an initial scan of certain library documents and policies, might last 30 to 45 minutes. Several days later, or whenever is mutually agreed on by the new employee and the mentor, the mentor will escort the new employee on a tour (or several mini-tours) of the library facility. Facilities tours and introduction of the new employee to staff outside of their immediate work area will be discussed in more detail in the next chapter. Prospective mentors should be assured that the time required is unlikely to be a hindrance to their regular job responsibilities, but if they should develop concern about possibly spending too much, or not enough, time in their mentoring role, they should discuss the matter with their supervisor or the NEO coordinator. It also is probably worth reminding workshop participants that before they will be approached to serve as mentors, the NEO coordinator will have sought and received approval from their supervisors.

Of all the duties and responsibilities assigned to the NEO mentor, if one had to be identified as the most important, it would probably be the need for the mentor to self-initiate contact with both the new employee and the NEO coordinator.

Regarding the mentor's interactions with the new employee, the mentor should not wrap up the first meeting with the remark, "Call me if you need anything." While telling the new employee to call if he or she needs anything is certainly appropriate, the mentor must not assume that not hearing from the new employee means the person doesn't have anything on his or her mind. In fact, most of us have been in positions at some time or another in which we did not ask questions because we did not know enough to ask a question! As established in the Introduction, a new employee is likely to be apprehensive about appearing dumb, fitting in, or being a bother. The mentor should be the one *reaching out* to the new employee during the first several weeks on the job to reassure the new employee that the mentor is, indeed, there for him or her.

Regarding self-initiated contacts with the NEO coordinator, mentors should be aware that this is particularly important if they sense anything wrong with their mentoring role, whether it be doubt about their doing a good job or a sense that they are not interacting well with the new employee. The NEO coordinator cannot help unless he or she knows that a problem may exist. To allow an uneasy feeling to go undiscussed sets the mentor and everyone else in the process up for a bigger problem, one that probably could have been dealt with earlier with just a little open discussion. Of course, the mentor (and NEO coordinator) should be reminded that one of the coordinator's duties and responsibilities is *also* to initiate frequent contact with all program participants.

How Mentors Are Selected: Unless covered earlier in the workshop during the program overview or the discussion about the duties and responsibilities of mentors, some brief mention should be made about how mentors are selected. As noted in Chapter 2, the NEO coordinator and new employee's immediate supervisor identify several possible mentor candidates, taking into consideration such factors as age, gender, general personality, and position of the new employee.

Discussion/Review of the NEO Mentor Checklist: Each staff member attending the workshop should be provided with a copy of the NEO mentor checklist. If organized as recommended in Chapter 2, the checklist will reinforce the program overview and clarify what the mentor should do when. It should be pointed out that the mentor checklist is very important in terms of documenting that a new employee has been provided with certain basic information and afforded opportunities to participate in activities that were felt to be appropriate for his or her orientation to the workplace. While it has not happened at ISU since the NEO program was implemented, it is certainly not beyond the realm of possibility that a new employee may at some point in the future turn out to be a problem employee. Written documentation regarding training and job-related information-sharing, as demonstrated on the various NEO checklists, may prove vital at some future time when disciplinary action has to be considered. While the mentor checklist is designed as a guide and aid to the mentor, workshop participants should understand that the checklist is not an optional component of the NEO mentoring process; all mentors, as well as immediate supervisors and the NEO coordinator, must maintain checklists designed specifically for their duties and responsibilities in the program. Upon completion of the NEO process, all checklists are collected by the NEO coordinator for NEO records.

Based on ISU's NEO experience, flexibility in maintaining the checklists should be expected and will be necessary depending on the uniqueness of any given new employee's orientation process. Making notes along checklist margins, and attaching additional sheets as necessary to provide relevant explanatory information about the mentor's interaction with the new employee, should be encouraged. Even though the checklist might imply certain rigid timelines (i.e., " . . . first day on the job," " . . . first, second, third week . . . ," etc.), these time periods are presented only as general guides.

Discussion/Review of Other Supporting Materials and Activities: Ideally, each workshop participant should be given his or her own copy of each major NEO document, with the obvious exception of the staff photo album and staff handbook, both discussed in detail in the next chapter. Understandably, photocopying time and expense may prohibit distribution of individual copies of all items. If individual copies of materials are not feasible, the NEO coordinator should circulate copies of documents to workshop participants after the workshop. At a minimum, a master list of all NEO support materials should be developed for participants to take with them after the workshop. If participants are not given their own copy of each supporting material, samples should be passed around for them to examine as each is being discussed. In addition to the staff photo album and staff handbook, NEO support materials might include a welcome packet, glossary of library terms and abbreviations, and library floor plans (each of these is discussed in the following chapter).

It is extremely important for the workshop instructor to stress that mentors are not required to be *content experts* for all the information collectively represented by the NEO supporting materials. Even the most knowledgeable among the veteran staff are not likely to recall the specific details of such things as funeral leave policies and emergency procedures to follow if the basement floods! What *should* be emphasized is that policies and procedures do exist for such situations, and procedures/policies are detailed and available in various documents and/or from other staff. Finally the workshop instructor should make an extra effort to let prospective mentors know that it's O.K. not to have the answer to every single question that may come from a new employee. As in traditional library reference work, mentors need not know all the answers, but they should know where to go for the answers, and that means knowing when to refer a question to someone else.

Discussion/Review of NEO Evaluation Procedures: Near the end of the workshop, the instructor should briefly discuss the importance of evaluation to the ultimate success of the program. The evaluation components of the NEO program should be identified and briefly reviewed—i.e., evaluation instruments designed for mentors, immediate supervisors, and new employees. Since some individuals tend to view evaluation as a negative, threatening process, rather than a positive process for improving performance, there may be employees who will become disinclined to be mentors if they will be personally evaluated by a peer-level new employee. In discussing the two evaluation instruments to be completed by the new employee (one after the first three weeks and one after the three-month probationary period), the workshop instructor should help employees understand that the new hire is being asked to evaluate the *NEO program,* not the performance of his or her mentor. Obviously, attention should also be given to the evaluation instrument designed for mentors to complete after they have served as a mentor for a new employee. A copy of the mentors' evaluation instrument should be provided for each workshop participant.

Miscellany: There are two other issues for workshop instructors to stress during the workshop:

1. That mentors should accentuate the positive in their interactions with the new employee.
2. How mentors should handle a poor mentor/employee match (discussed in Chapter 3).

The workshop instructor might acknowledge that it is simply human nature to have personal biases, likes, dislikes, viewpoints, and opinions. In a library, there will be staff who acknowledge and follow certain policies and procedures without necessarily agreeing with them or approving of them on a personal level. Further, some staff do better than others at keeping their personal viewpoints about work policies to themselves. Prospective mentors should be encouraged to avoid consciously injecting their personal

> It is extremely important for the workshop instructor to stress that mentors are not required to be content experts for all the information collectively represented by the NEO supporting materials.

biases into the presentation, discussion, and interpretation of any library policies or procedures. Leave the new employee to come to his or her own opinion. Likewise, it is only human nature that in interacting with others in the workplace we tend to develop certain opinions about co-workers— some we like, some we dislike; some we enjoy and respect, others we try to avoid. In order to be successful and productive in the workplace, like it or not, everyone is forced to interact and work cooperatively with one another regardless of any negative interpersonal feelings about co-workers. Again, some individuals will do a better job than others at separating their less positive personal perceptions about co-workers when interacting with a new employee. An effective way during the mentor training workshop to underscore the importance of this issue is to point out to mentors that their engaging in negative discussions of co-workers or library policy could easily result in a new employee coming to the less-than-positive conclusion that the mentor is a gossip, not a team player, and is, therefore, someone to be avoided in the future. In the mentor/new employee relationship, personal perceptions will certainly work both ways.

Finally, there is always the possibility that a mentor and new employee will be incompatible at an interpersonal level—i.e., they just do not get along. Luckily, this problem has not come up at ISU to any great extent; however, the possibility has always been recognized. Since the possibility of a mismatch does exist, it is important that both the new employee and the mentor be advised about how to handle the situation should it arise. As discussed in Chapter 3, the NEO coordinator should have already set the stage for handling this problem by openly discussing the possibility with both the new employee and the mentor during his or her first meeting with each. While the NEO coordinator should not belabor the point, he or she must make it clear to both that if a problem seems to exist or seems to be developing, the key to solving it is immediate communication with the coordinator and/or immediate supervisor. The new employee and mentor should understand that the NEO coordinator is available either to help resolve any problems or diplomatically dissolve the relationship. The NEO coordinator should also stress that fault or blame for the incompatibility would not be a matter of concern. Again, early communication of a mismatch problem, initiated by either the new employee or the mentor, is key to handling this situation.

As in the previous discussion suggests, the mentor training workshop should involve a variety of methods for presenting information to those attending. At least initially, the mentor training workshops are likely to be a bit two-dimensional and theoretical since the NEO coordinator and/or program developer(s) will be the individuals with the clearest understanding of what the mentoring role is intended to be. As has been illustrated, training workshops offered at the outset of the NEO program can easily incorporate overhead transparencies, slides, flip charts, or other media designed to clarify key points regarding the overall NEO program, the relationships between participants, and practical tips for being a good mentor. Handouts for distribution to workshop participants should include, at a minimum, the goals of the NEO program, the duties and responsibilities of the NEO mentor, the mentor's checklist, and the evaluation instrument designed for completion by mentors after they have participated in the program. Given the numbers of handouts appropriate for distribution to prospective mentors, the NEO coordinator might want to consider organizing these materials into some type of NEO mentor's handbook.

After the NEO program has been in existence for some time, an identifiable experience-based body of information will develop that will address more specifically such areas as the questions most frequently asked by new employees; which activities/materials work and which do not seem to work as well in the orientation process; and how much time mentoring actually takes. Collecting this information, and successfully incorporating it into the program, is a major responsibility of the NEO coordinator. After several months, mentor training workshops could incorporate testimonials from veteran mentors and fairly recent new employees who had particularly good mentoring experiences during their orientation period. Role-playing activities based on real NEO mentoring experiences might also be developed for the training workshops to reinforce the dynamics of the mentor/new employee relationship. Finally, individuals who have demonstrated their abilities and enthusiasm for serving as NEO mentors could even be given responsibility for conducting all or portions of the mentor training workshops, thereby lessening some of the load that heretofore has fallen on the NEO coordinator.

An evaluation component should be included in planning and organizing the mentor training workshop. Develop an evaluation instrument to be administered to participants shortly after their attendance at a training workshop. Since administering the evaluation immediately after, or shortly after, the workshop requires mentor trainees to evaluate their training before applying it in practice, the final mentor evaluation (administered after having served as a mentor) should include one or more questions about the mentor training workshop they attended, and its adequacy in terms of

> Handouts for distribution to workshop participants should include, at a minimum, the goals of the NEO program, the duties and responsibilities of the NEO mentor, the mentor's checklist, and the evaluation instrument designed for completion by mentors after they have participated in the program.

preparing them to be mentors. Both types of evaluation information should be sought (e.g., right after the workshop *and* after serving as a mentor), since those completing their mentor roles are several months removed from the workshop experience and may not be able to be very specific in making suggestions about the workshop if only asked long after the fact.

THE WELCOME LETTER

Input from employees who have gone through ISU's New Employee Orientation program clearly indicates that one of the most positive and most appreciated aspects of the whole NEO program was the welcome letter they received a few days before starting the job. The welcome letter is a brief, personalized letter sent to the new employee's home address just prior to his or her starting date. The letter should be informal, almost conversational in tone and style. To adopt a formal tone and style would do little to calm the normal apprehension and anxiety of a soon-to-be new employee. Informality is not compromised by the letter being typed and printed on official institutional letterhead. In fact, the combination of letterhead/word-processing, and conversational style subtly makes formal more comfortable.

There may be some value in drafting different versions of welcome letters for support staff and library faculty/professional staff. For instance, welcome letters for new professional employees might make specific references to assisting the new employee in understanding library governance, opportunities for staff development, or performance evaluation procedures. Another reason for developing multiple versions of the welcome letter is to minimize the possibility (as unlikely as it may be) that two new employees might compare notes and discover that the personalized letters they received were, in fact, not so personal. As noted earlier, saving multiple versions of word-processed welcome letters as electronic files makes generating them in the future fast and simple.

The welcome letter could be sent by someone in the library's top administration (director, dean, department head, etc.), by the new hire's immediate supervisor, or by the NEO coordinator. At ISU, the welcome letter is sent by the NEO coordinator. But regardless of who sends it, the welcome letter should be a line item on the NEO coordinator's checklist so that he or she makes sure that it is drafted and mailed so that the new employee receives it just

The welcome letter is a brief, informal, personalized letter sent to the new employee's home address just prior to his or her starting date.

prior to his or her first day on the job. And as noted in the previous chapter about the problem of the NEO coordinator getting short notice of a new employee's arrival on the job, if there is not enough lead time to send a letter, a personal telephone call can serve equally well in letting a new employee know that he or she is eagerly expected.

Note in the sample letters (figs. 4-2 and 4-3) that copies have been sent to all key participants. These copies serve as good reminders about the new employee's arrival and everyone's upcoming role in the orientation process.

ASSEMBLING SUPPORT MATERIALS

Since the NEO coordinator is likely to be someone who wears many hats, administrative efficiency is of particular importance. In this and preceding chapters, several key pieces of NEO documentation have been identified or alluded to, among them checklists for mentors and supervisors, a specialized glossary of library terms and abbreviations, evaluation instruments for all participants, and a library staff handbook. A considerable amount of the NEO coordinator's administrative time can be saved if core materials are preassembled into a generic master file, ready and waiting when the NEO coordinator receives word that a new employee will be joining the library staff. The benefits of preassembling materials will be most apparent during those occasional periods of high turnover and short notice of a new employee's arrival identified in Chapter 3. The two chapters that follow provide a detailed discussion of several major support materials not yet covered.

MEETINGS WITH THE IMMEDIATE SUPERVISOR AND MENTOR

As this chapter suggests, a great deal of responsibility falls on the NEO coordinator prior to a new employee's start date. Even though the NEO program options described in this book provide a general framework for addressing the orientation needs of all new em-

FIGURE 4-2 STAFF LETTER

Tuesday, January 26, 1993

Ms. Jane Smith
725 E. 35th St.
Clinton, Indiana 47842

Dear Ms. Smith:

As coordinator of Indiana State University Libraries' New Employee Orientation (NEO) program, I am writing to say "Welcome aboard!" The Libraries' NEO program is a rather informal information-sharing program designed to help all new library employees get settled into their new positions. The program helps you become aware of library facilities and services, introduces you to library staff outside of your immediate work area, and calls attention to basic library policies and procedures. I will be getting in touch shortly after you begin work to talk more about the NEO program.

I look forward to meeting with you next week and working with you at Indiana State University Libraries.

Sincerely,

H. Scott Davis, Ed.D.
Head, Library Instruction & Orientation
and NEO Program Coordinator

cc: Joan Evans, Administrative Assistant I   *[Note: New employee's immediate supervisor]*
    Nancy Watkins, Library Assistant I and NEO Mentor

ployees, the orientation process for each new employee joining the library staff will require some individualized planning and organization. As soon as the NEO coordinator is notified of a new employee's start date, he or she should schedule a meeting with the new employee's immediate supervisor. As outlined in the NEO coordinator's checklist presented and discussed in Chapter 2, the NEO coordinator and immediate supervisor must discuss various factors relating to the position that is being filled. Since the immediate supervisor presumably has met and interacted with the

---

FIGURE 4-3 FACULTY LETTER

Tuesday, January 26, 1993

Mr. John Doe
642 E. Riley St.
Atlanta, GA 47842

Dear Mr. Doe:

As coordinator of Indiana State University Libraries' New Employee Orientation (NEO) program, I am writing to welcome you to the ISU Library faculty. The Libraries' NEO program is a rather informal information-sharing program designed to help all new library employees get settled into their new positions. The program will help you become aware of library facilities and services, will introduce you to library staff outside of your immediate work area, and will call attention to basic library policies and procedures.

The NEO program will provide you with opportunities to interact with your new colleagues for discussion of any questions you may have regarding the tenure process, service, research and publication. A wide range of expertise and professional involvement is represented in ISU's library faculty. We are all ready to assist you in any way we can.

I will be contacting you shortly after you begin work to talk more about the NEO program; however, in the meantime, should you have any questions or need any assistance as you prepare to join us, please do not hesitate to contact me. I look forward to meeting with you personally next week and working with you at Indiana State University Libraries.

Sincerely,

H. Scott Davis, Ed.D.
Head, Library Instruction & Orientation
 and NEO Program Coordinator

cc: Ron Martin, Associate Dean, Library Public Services *[Note: New employee's immediate supervisor]*
     Marsha Miller, Instruction Librarian and NEO Mentor

---

new employee as part of the interview process, the coordinator should let the supervisor take the lead in selecting mentor candidates and identifying any unique informational needs of the new employee based on the requirements of the position. Regarding mentor selection, the coordinator must be aware of who has gone through mentor training and is available to serve as a mentor. If a mentor candidate who has not participated in a training workshop is preferred by both the supervisor and the NEO coordinator and another mentor workshop is not scheduled before the new employee's start date, if time permits, the coordinator will have to provide individualized mentor training. In addition to the activities already identified on his or her checklist, the immediate supervisor should also set up a schedule for the new employee for the first few days on the job. The NEO coordinator should work with the immediate supervisor to schedule a block of time for his or her initial meeting with the new employee. Ideally, this meeting should be scheduled on the new employee's first day. Throughout the meeting with the supervisor, the NEO coordinator should take notes on those things that will need to be incorporated into participants' checklists or shared with the mentor, e.g., special information needs, the need for any special presenters, general information about the new employee, etc.

After meeting with the new employee's immediate supervisor, the NEO coordinator contacts the supervisor of the first-choice mentor candidate to get approval for the candidate to serve as a mentor (*see* Chapter 2). After getting supervisory approval, the coordinator then approaches the mentor candidate to see if he or she is available and willing to serve as a mentor within the specific timeframe. Depending on how much time has passed since the mentor candidate participated in a mentor training workshop, an initial informal meeting is scheduled for the NEO coordinator to meet with the mentor candidate to review the basics of the mentoring process and to share information about the individual who will be joining the staff. The coordinator should also go ahead and schedule the initial meeting between the mentor and the new employee.

After meeting with the new employee's immediate supervisor and getting a mentor commitment, the NEO coordinator must next set up all the appropriate checklists for distribution to participants prior to the new employee's start date. The coordinator should allow several days leadtime before the new employee's first day to give the immediate supervisor and the mentor enough time to review their checklists and planned activities. Then, just prior to the new employee's start date, all three participants should get together to review materials, confirm meeting dates and times, and deal with any last-minute questions.

5 INITIAL ACTIVITIES AND MATERIALS

In planning and organizing the different types of information and activities that should be shared with a new employee during his or her orientation, consideration should be given to the information-overload factor. During his or her first few days and weeks, a new employee is typically inundated with more information than can be processed and retained. Depending on the individual, this feeling of overload can quickly result in stress, a general sense of panic, and anxiety about his or her ability to perform the job. Such feelings are counter to the goals of an NEO program. Careful organization, planning, and delivery/presentation of materials and activities, and openly letting the new employee know that you and others are sensitive to his or her being bombarded with a lot of information, can significantly decrease or eliminate any negative fallout from too much information too soon.

In keeping with this, when setting up the initial schedule for the new employee, the NEO coordinator and immediate supervisor should incorporate a few blocks of time each day or every other day of the first week or two for the new employee to read and review the various materials that are provided. If possible, the supervisor, NEO coordinator, mentor, and/or knowledgeable co-worker of the new employee should be available during these times to answer any questions or clarify areas that may not be clear to the new employee. Or the new employee could be asked to jot down any questions that he or she might have in the course of reviewing the materials. Answering these questions could be the basis for one or more informal meetings later between the new employee and his or her mentor, supervisor, or the NEO coordinator.

In addition to the support activities and materials discussed in this chapter, there are several miscellaneous housekeeping chores that can easily fall through the cracks during an employee's first few days on the job. Depending on your library's situation, any or all of the following items may need to be given consideration: staff identification card; building/office keys; parking permit, map, regulations; getting new employee's name, position, office number, phone number, etc., added to various campus (and library) directories, mailing lists, or routing lists; assignment of any required system/network passwords or account names; and issuing a staff locker. Finally, many libraries have internal publications for staff. Quite often there are also staff publications produced by a library's parent organization intended for a wider staff audience than just the library—i.e., school systems for school libraries, universities for academic libraries, staff newsletters for special libraries, and city/county staff publications for public libraries. Many of these publications typically include brief announcements or biographical sketches about new staff. Blurbs of appropriate length should be drafted by the NEO coordinator or designee about new library employees and forwarded to any such publications just before, or shortly after, new employees' arrivals. These are just a few of the typical "loose ends" that may need to be taken care of as soon as possible. The NEO coordinator, immediate supervisor, and mentor should discuss any of the preceding types of items that might apply to any given new employee's situation and divvy up among

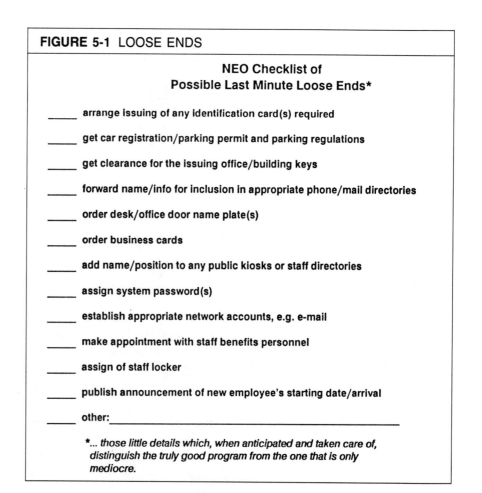

FIGURE 5-1 LOOSE ENDS

NEO Checklist of
Possible Last Minute Loose Ends*

_____ arrange issuing of any identification card(s) required

_____ get car registration/parking permit and parking regulations

_____ get clearance for the issuing office/building keys

_____ forward name/info for inclusion in appropriate phone/mail directories

_____ order desk/office door name plate(s)

_____ order business cards

_____ add name/position to any public kiosks or staff directories

_____ assign system password(s)

_____ establish appropriate network accounts, e.g. e-mail

_____ make appointment with staff benefits personnel

_____ assign of staff locker

_____ publish announcement of new employee's starting date/arrival

_____ other:_____

*... those little details which, when anticipated and taken care of, distinguish the truly good program from the one that is only mediocre.

themselves who will take care of what. In cases requiring the new employee to go to an office outside of the library, someone should accompany him or her if at all possible.

THE WELCOME PACKET

At ISU, *Welcome Packet* is the collective term given to those materials that are presented to the new employee during his or her first meeting with the NEO coordinator. The welcome packet is one of two keystones of the orientation-related information given to a new employee. How much and what to include in the welcome packet will vary depending on a new employee's position, the amount of library or related experience he or she brings to the job, and his or her familiarity with the community/area where the library is physically located (in the case of ISU or other academic libraries, the campus).

In soliciting staff input during the developmental stages of an NEO program (*see* Chapter 1), specific suggestions should be sought regarding what would be appropriate to include in a welcome packet for any new library employee. At ISU, the staff surveys administered during initial program development included questions that addressed this issue. The result of staff input yielded a core of materials appropriate to any new library staff position. While some materials had to be created from scratch, many of the items recommended by staff already existed as part of some library program or service—e.g., instructional/information handouts, brochures, etc. Other materials were developed by shifting the audience perspective of existing materials from "library user" to "new library employee."

Similar to the checklists developed for use by the NEO coordinator, mentor, and supervisor, a checklist of welcome packet contents could be developed once the initial core is identified. This checklist would then be used by the NEO coordinator or whoever is given the responsibility for assembling the welcome packet. At ISU, the assistant to the NEO coordinator (who is also head of library instruction and orientation) pulls together welcome packet materials prior to each new employee's arrival. The welcome packet checklist shown identifies the major components of the ISU welcome packet for new employees.

The welcome packet is one of two keystones of all the orientation-related information given to the new employee.

FIGURE 5-2 WELCOME PACKET CHECKLIST

New Employee: _____ Start Date: _____

Position: _____ Department/Unit: _____

New to ISU? Yes   No   (If not new to ISU, check all that apply:)

    Current/recent ISU student: _____   Former student assistant: Library _____   Other: _____

    Current/recent ISU non-library staff position: _____

Welcome Packet contents (place appropriate items in labeled folder, forward to NEO Coordinator):

    ___ NEO Program Rationale and Goals

    ___ *Glossary of Common Library Terms and Abbreviations*

    ___ *Indiana State University Libraries Staff Handbook* -- request from Staff Development
        Committee (contents); send to Processing for name personalization on cover

    ___ *ISU Library Faculty Handbook* (for new Library faculty only) -- request from LFA Secretary

    ___ Library calendar (academic year calendar showing all holidays, when Libraries are open,
        etc.);

    ___ current Library staff phone list

    ___ Information about Library Staff Association (form letter in file)

    ___ Information about Library Faculty Assembly (for faculty members only)

    ___ Hulman Memorial Student Union information

    ___ *Guide to Indiana State University Libraries* brochure with all informational inserts;

    ___ diagrams of Main Library floors

    ___ copies of current instructional materials specific to LUIS III, LIBNET and any other
        instructional materials relevant to new employee's position (standard items include: Self-
        paced Tour; LC Class.; Brief Guides to LUIS III, LUIS, WILI, ERIC, DION; LIBNET; Using
        Libnet; CD-ROMs at ISU; Lib. Locations/Getting Help...)

        Other: _____

        _____

    ___ *ISU Libraries NewsLine* (most recent issue)

    ___ Information/user's manual for campus e-mail system

    ___ Information on LAN (request from LAN Administrator)

Additional Items: _____

_____

                                Welcome Packet assembled by _____
                                                          Initials/Date

LIBRARY STAFF HANDBOOK

A library staff handbook is the other keystone of the information provided a new employee during his or her first few days on the job. Whether a library system decides to offer a new employee orientation program or not, all libraries should have some form of staff handbook outlining the basic institutional/library policies and procedures that govern each staff member's day-to-day employment. A well-produced staff handbook should provide at least partial answers to any questions or job-related concerns a new employee might have and identify more detailed resources or resource persons for information beyond that which is provided in the handbook.

Developing and maintaining a good staff handbook constitute a big job—pulling together the information appropriate for a staff handbook is usually fairly easy compared to organizing the information in a way that makes it easily and quickly accessible. The physical organization of the handbook should include a complete table of contents and more importantly, a keyword index. At ISU, the Library Staff Development Committee (*see* Chapter 3), under the guidance and approval of the library administration, oversees the upkeep, physical production, and distribution of updates of the *ISU Libraries Staff Handbook*. The NEO coordinator handles distribution of the handbook to all new employees. A sample table of contents modeled after that of the ISU handbook is included to show examples of major sections and the types of information included in the handbook.

Many of the entries in the *ISU Libraries Staff Handbook* of a policy nature actually cite the full policy on the topic. However, it should be noted that in many instances, a handbook entry for a particular topic may be very brief, citing a more thorough, exhaustive, and/or definitive source for more detailed information. For example, in ISU's handbook the actual handbook entry for "General Policies Manual for Student Assistants" under "Library Policies and Procedures" does not include the complete student assistant manual which is approximately 20 pages. Instead, the handbook entry is designed to let the staff member know that such a manual exists by simply stating that the student assistant manual is " . . . a library-generated manual given to all new student assistants before or during their general orientation session, to acquaint them with the library, similar in function to this Staff Handbook. These manuals are available from the Dept. of Library Instruction & Orientation." In this regard, a library staff handbook should

---

FIGURE 5-3 SAMPLE TABLE OF CONTENTS FOR STAFF HANDBOOK

Preface . . . .

Library Organizational Chart . . . .

Library Policies and Procedures . . . .

Attendance at Meetings	Library Staff Development
Breaks	Mail
Convenience Days	Photocopying
Emergencies	Sick Leave
Funeral Leave	Vacation Leave
Holidays	Workman's Compensation

University & Library Handbooks/Manuals . . . .

Disaster/Salvage Information and Emergency Plan	Administrative Policies Manual
Emergency and Security Guidelines	Preservation Plan
General Policies Manual for Student Assistants	Staff Employee's Hanbook
Glossary of Common Library Terms and Abbreviations	University Faculty Handbook

University/Library-related Publications/Minutes . . . .

University (non-Library):

Academic Notes	*Healthwise*
Alumni Newsletter	*Infobits*
Faculty Senate Minutes	Office Personnel Council Minutes
Fall Greetings	*Update*

Library:

CML Announcements	Library Faculty Assembly Minutes
CML Bulletin	*Library NewsLine*
Dept. Heads' Meetings Minutes	Library Systems Monthly Summary

Library Forms . . . .

Absentee Reports	Request for (Annual/Vacation) Leave
Employer's Report of Injury	Rush Request (for Library Materials)
Plan for Taking Course Work	Supply Request
Purchase Request Form (PRF)	Travel Request (for Professional Leave/Funding)

Library Organizations . . . .

Friends of the Library	Office Personnel Council (OPC) Representatives
Library Faculty Assembly (LFA)	Support Staff Representatives to Dean
Library Staff Association (LSA)	Miscellaneous State, National, and Professional Organizations

--continued on next page--

FIGURE 5-3 CONTINUED

Major Library Committees . . . .

Collection Development Advisory Comm. (CDAC)   Staff Development Committee
CML EDitorial Board   Systems Advisory Committee (SAC)
Display Committee

Miscellany . . . .

Change Machines   New Employee Orientation (NEO) Programs
Cot Room   Portable Personal Computers
Faculty Word Processing Center   Staff Lockers
First Aid Kit   Staff Lounge
Journal Routing   Telephone Books
Library Information Rack   Tools

**Brief Descriptions of Departments,
Branches and Units** . . . .

History of Indiana State University Libraries . . . .

Index . . . .

Appendix of Sample Forms

Absentee Report   Request for Leave
Employer's Report of Injury   Rush Request
Plan for Taking Coursework   Supply Request
Purchase Request Form (PRF)

Miscellaneous Notes, Updates, etc.

---

be viewed in some ways as a directory of other documents. In the example just cited, if a new employee's job involved a significant amount of student assistant supervision, he or she would know from the staff handbook entry to contact the Department of Library Instruction and Orientation for copies of the manual or for more background about the student assistant manual's development and use. Of course, if the new employee's position involves the supervision of student assistants, an actual student assistant's policy manual could be included in his or her Welcome Packet.

GLOSSARY OF LIBRARY TERMS AND ABBREVIATIONS

Like all professions, librarianship is not without its own jargon. For the totally new employee with little or no practical work experience in a library, bombardment with some of the words, phrases, and abbreviations that veteran staff take for granted can be very intimidating during the first few days and weeks on the job. Depending on the level of past experience brought to the job by a new employee, the supervisor should remind co-workers in the new employee's immediate work area to be particularly mindful of their use of jargon when interacting with the new employee.

A good way of helping a new employee learn the library's lingo is to develop a specialized glossary that includes frequently used words and abbreviations that any library staff member, regardless of particular position or title, should be familiar with. Such glossaries have been used successfully in business in orienting new employees. A library glossary for new employees should include not only the words, phrases, and abbreviations that tend to be universally understood by members of the library profession but also any local jargon unique to the particular library situation.

The initial development of a library glossary can be a rather ominous task. Developing a first draft is a good group project, perhaps for a staff development committee. Here are some practical suggestions for developing a glossary of library terms and abbreviations:

Brainstorm a list of possible glossary entries, then share the list with others for their additions and suggestions: Ask others to develop their own list of terms and abbreviations that they think would be helpful to a new employee. Be sure to include in this brainstorming process staff members from all divisions (technical and public services), from all classifications (professional and nonprofessional), and various levels of experience. Soliciting glossary entry suggestions as a part of a library staff survey is another excellent way to identify appropriate words, phrases, and abbreviations (*see* Survey Sample II in Chapter 1).

Resist the urge to be unnecessarily inclusive: There is no absolute formula about what should be included in a specialized glossary. However, if the glossary becomes overly detailed or in-

A library glossary for new employees should include not only the words, phrases, and abbreviations that tend to be universally understood by members of the library profession but also any local jargon that is unique to the particular library situation.

cludes too many entries, it's effect may turn out to be the opposite of that intended: The new employee may experience anxiety and stress from the information overload. So be selective about what you include. Avoid extremely job-specific terminology. Remember that the glossary should be generic, including only those terms and abbreviations that should be familiar to all library staff.

Develop the glossary for the new employee with little or no previous library work experience: At any point in time, the range of experience among an entire library staff will vary from many years of experience to limited or practically no experience. Even though one runs the risk of insulting the intelligence of those new hires with considerable library experience, a new employee glossary should be developed for the least experienced new employee in terms of library work experience; otherwise, the glossary becomes impractical. A glossary developed with the most experienced in mind would serve only to confuse new employees and/or falsely confirm any fears they may be having about their adequacy for the position. If multiple versions of the glossary are attempted, those responsible for development and revisions are likely to discover that variations in work experience among new employees are unpredictable. The amount of work involved in creating and maintaining multiple versions of the glossary also will quickly outweigh the benefits of having several versions of specialized glossaries based on staff experience levels.

Solicit Drafts of Definitions for Use in the Final Glossary from Those Individuals on Staff with the Most Knowledge and Expertise in that Particular Area: The individual or group responsible for drafting a library glossary should not expect to come up with all the definitions without assistance from others. The profession is a complex one with many areas of specialization and expertise. Go to the in-house experts for input. They will appreciate your acknowledgement of their expertise and the opportunity to participate. But to avoid long-winded or overly technical definitions, provide a few basic guidelines for those drafting the entries. For example, suggest that entry drafts should be about 30 words or less, be developed for a beginning library employee with no experience, and be free of jargon or technical terms. Remind writers that the purpose of the glossary is to put unfamiliar terminology and jargon into an understandable context for the new employee who may hear a term in work conversation or see it in print. Al-

> . . . if the glossary becomes overly detailed or includes too many entries, its effect may turn out to be the opposite of that intended: The new employee may experience anxiety and stress from information overload.

The glossary's purpose is to inform generally, not to educate the reader in all facets of the entry.

ways reserve the right to final edit! The glossary's purpose is to inform generally, not to educate its reader in all facets of the entry. Finally, be sure to acknowledge the experts' contributions to the glossary somewhere in the introduction.

Glossary Entries Should Reflect Our Own Tools of the Trade: In addition to simple definitions, entries should include appropriate *see* and *see also* references to other glossary terms and abbreviations that are related or that might clarify the new employee's understanding of the entry. Pronunciation information is also desirable, particularly about acronyms and abbreviations. Pronunciation information need not require a phonetic character set. As shown in the sample abbreviation section, pronunciation notes can be made up of pronounceable words and syllables.

Keep the format and layout simple: ISU's glossary is organized into separate terms and abbreviations sections, each in alphabetic order. Use double spacing between entries, indention, bold type, and/or italics to facilitate scanning. Depending on the length of the final draft, incorporate running heads at the top of each page to further facilitate reader access. Include a brief introductory note explaining the glossary's purpose and encouraging new employees to seek clarification when they encounter new terminology on the job. Provide blank space at the end of each section or at the end of the glossary so new employees can make notes and add items not included in the glossary. Ask new employees to forward these terms as they are found to the NEO coordinator, staff development committee, or whoever is responsible for updating the glossary. Spiral bind or staple the glossary pages for distribution. Include a cover sheet of heavier paper stock, perhaps in an attractive color. Incorporating clip art, original artwork, or modified artwork on the glossary's cover and/or throughout the text will add visual interest to the layout. Depending on the desired overall tone one wishes to achieve with the glossary, humor may be injected at this point. The illustration shown has been used on the front cover of all revisions òf ISU's glossary, with only minor updating of the copy in the conversation box. If the cartoon looks somewhat familiar, it is because it is based on an illustration included in *ALA Library Clip Art* (1983). White typing correction fluid allowed the NEO coordinator to change the original facial expression of the person behind the desk from friendly/self-assured to seemingly dumb-founded by the patron's question. A felt tip

---

FIGURE 5-4 SAMPLE GLOSSARY ENTRIES

EXCERPT FROM GLOSSARY'S LIBRARY TERMS SECTION

Glossary of Library Terms (continued)

fax: slang for telefacsimile.

frontend: that part of the computer software which the user interacts with, usually making it easier to use the computer system.

full-text database: collection of computerized data which includes the entire text of journal articles, books, etc. Examples at ISU Libraries include *Business Dateline*, a CD-ROM which contains the text of almost 200 regional business journals, and the *New Electronic Encyclopedia*, also a CD-ROM database. See also *CD-ROM, CD-ROM Network,* and *LIBNET.*

gateway: computer software which allows one to use one computer system to connect with another, usually distant, computer system.

EXCERPT FROM GLOSSARY'S LIBRARY ABBREVIATIONS SECTION

ALA - DTP

Glossary of Library Abbreviations (continued)

ALA (not pronounced, spelled out A-L-A): American Library Association; major national organization for professional librarians; ALA holds two conferences per year which many ISU librarians attend: midwinter conference (in January) and national conference (usually in June).

BI (pronounced BEE EYE): the traditional slang for bibliographic, or library, instruction.

CDAC (pronounced SEE-DACK): Collection Development Advisory Committee; a standing library committee that makes recommendations specific to library collections, e.g. purchase of new materials, subscription cancellations, etc.

CD-ROM (spelled out and pronounced C-D-RAHM): Compact Disc-Read Only Memory; an electronic format used in the library for storage and retrieval of print information; a single small, silver CD can hold the equivalent of approximately 175,000 - 200,000 pages of print information. ISU Libraries has several CD-ROM databases available in the Reference Department and the Science Library. See also *CD-ROM Network.*

pen and minimal artistic ability allowed for the insertion of the conversation box and the printout being held by the patron. Note that the conversation box incorporates numerous terms of the profession and ISU Libraries' unique local lingo. Library-specific clip art books are available through ALA publishing. There are also numerous sources of commercially produced clip art, though some tend to be rather expensive.

Finally, be sure to add a date somewhere within the glossary, either on the front cover, at the end of the introduction, and/or

Regardless of price and origin, clip art can be put to many creative uses in other library publications.

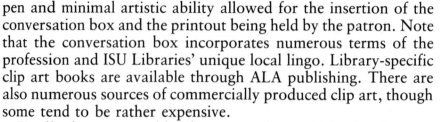

FIGURE 5-5 GLOSSARY FRONT COVER WITH CARTOON

GLOSSARY

of Common Library Terms and Abbreviations

New Employee Orientation (NEO) Program

Indiana State University Libraries

at the very end of the text; this will make distinction between subsequent revisions much less frustrating for glossary users.

Field test the prototype: After a draft has been developed, share it with library staff, both veterans and new hires, to get their critical reaction prior to its wholesale production and distribution. If certain suggestions crop up several times, heed the collective input! There is likely something wrong with an entry that is identified as problematic by several individuals in a field test.

Make the first edition of the glossary available to all library staff: In surveying library staff at ISU during the developmental stages of the NEO program, 100 percent of those surveyed agreed that a glossary of library terms would be helpful to any new library staff member. The survey also included a list of 40 library terms or abbreviations and asked staff to indicate how many of the items they felt they could briefly define in one or two sentences. Twenty-eight of the 40 were the average number of terms/ abbreviations that staff felt they could define. Results of this exercise tend to reinforce the earlier assumption regarding how much we take for granted about what we know (and don't know). In a follow-up item on the same staff survey, 91 percent of respondents indicated that they thought a glossary of library terms and abbreviations would be of practical value to *all* library staff, not just new hires.

There are several ways of making the glossary available for its intended audience. In response to staff input, the first edition of the ISU glossary was distributed to all library staff as a separate document. Subsequent revisions of the glossary are now included as a distinct document in the NEO welcome packet for new employees and are also made available to veteran library staff.

Make provisions for future revisions: Terms and abbreviations will come and go over time. Annual or biennial revisions of the glossary will probably be sufficient; more frequent revisions can be handled by distributing addenda. From the first use of a new employee glossary, all staff should be encouraged to forward corrections and suggestions at any point in time. As revisions are produced and distributed, those receiving the revised editions should be told to destroy or recycle the earlier edition.

INTRODUCTIONS TO STAFF OUTSIDE THE IMMEDIATE WORK AREA

Some people are blessed, others cursed, when it comes to remembering the names of people to whom they have been introduced only once or twice. Regardless of a new employee's personal ability at name recall, the fact that he or she is being loaded down with so much information during the first few days on the job makes it very likely that he or she would appreciate help in learning the names of library staff. Of course, the overall size of a library's staff will determine the extent to which this situation may or may not be a problem.

There are several things that can be included as part of the NEO program to assist new employees in remembering the names of those to whom they have been introduced. Name tags for all library staff can do much to ease the awkwardness of forgetting someone's name. In some libraries, name tags are considered part of daily work attire. However, considerable controversy surrounds name tags among many in the profession. Without getting bogged down in the particulars of the controversy, suffice it to say that some library staff members feel uneasy about indiscriminately identifying themselves to library patrons for fear of receiving harassing phone calls or being stalked. Regardless, name tags do have a positive side from a new employee's perspective.

Another way to deal with introductions of a new employee to existing staff is to openly acknowledge with the new employee that name recognition and recall are unsettling problems that most people struggle with at one time or another. Veteran library staff should be reminded to *initiate* their own introductions during their first couple of interactions with a new employee. The new employee should also be encouraged to ask a staff member his or her name if the staff member should fail to offer it first.

Finally, introductions and remembering staff names can be greatly facilitated by producing a staff photo album. At ISU, the NEO staff photo album has been a tremendous success.

STAFF PHOTO ALBUM

Although it involves some planning and expense, a library staff photo album is both a practical and beneficial (not to mention entertaining) item to include as a standard resource in an NEO program. It does much to reinforce personal introductions before and after the fact. A new employee can easily review the photo section for a particular unit or department just prior to a tour of that area. Or shortly after being introduced to staff in a department or unit, a new staff member can informally test his or her recall by reviewing names and faces in the album. A staff photo album will also be beneficial for veteran staff, particularly those who work in relatively isolated areas or in libraries with very large staffs or branch facilities.

A staff photo album can be effectively produced in-house at minimal expense. The following production tips are based on ISU's experience and will help ensure a top-notch album:

Responsibility for production and upkeep: The initial production of a staff photo album can be somewhat time-consuming. Unfortunately, during periods of high staff turnover, keeping a staff photo album up-to-date can be equally time-consuming if a specific individual, department, or committee is not designated as responsible for its upkeep. Regardless of who is responsible, the NEO coordinator should monitor the currency and accuracy of the staff album. At ISU, production of the first staff photo album was assigned to a graduate intern working for academic credits in the library instruction department. Upkeep of the album over the past several years has been the responsibility of the library instruction office assistant.

Physical organization and layout: A standard three-ring loose leaf binder format is highly recommended. Binders are available that have a clear plastic insert over the entire front cover. This allows for inexpensive customizing and occasionally a change in cover design. The adhesive photo album pages make updates quick and also allow flexibility in experimenting with the actual layout of pictures. Introductory pages (title page, table of contents, introductory/purpose statement, etc.) and an index should also be included.

> [A staff photo album] does much to reinforce personal introductions before and after the fact.

Organize content by division (public services, technical services, etc.) and by department/unit within divisions. This organization should be reflected in the album's table of contents. If one exists for your library, include an organization chart that illustrates the administrative structure and lines of report within the library system. Include two indexes: an alphabetically arranged list of all staff names (including their department affiliation and position title), and a list of departments/units within the main library divisions with staff assigned to each area. Pages should be numbered. Like the glossary, humor can be incorporated into a staff photo album depending on the desired tone.

Use of a timeline and shot sheet: Knowing what pictures are needed *before* starting to take photos will save a lot of time when it comes to putting the photo album together. First, develop a shot sheet. A shot sheet is a checklist of every shot that is needed. For each picture listed on the shot sheet, an abbreviation indicating the type of shot to be taken should be noted, i.e. CU = close up, MS = midshot, and LS = long shot (*see Composing and taking the shots,* below). In addition to assuring that the photographer will get all the shots needed, a shot sheet is an important tool for estimating costs of production. Given an approximate total number of needed photos, cost calculations can be made, i.e., number of rolls of film for required exposures plus cost of film processing for that many rolls. Since it may be desirable to have at least two copies of a staff photo album (or perhaps more, depending on overall staff size and annual turnover), another cost consideration is the price of duplicate processed prints, this should be included in overall production cost estimates.

The shot sheet should be organized in such a way that pictures that will be taken in the same general area of the library are grouped together on the list. Blank lines should be included in each departmental section so the photographer can make note of any unplanned additional shots taken.

Once a shot sheet has been prepared, a timeline should be developed indicating which pictures will be taken when. Chances are that picture-taking will take several days, particularly in large libraries with branches. In developing the timeline, the NEO coordinator, or whoever is actually serving as photographer for the album, should contact department heads and/or office supervisors well in advance to arrange his or her visit. Supervisors will be able to identify the least disruptive times for such a visit, and also will be able to advise on staff vacations, known absences, etc. After a timeline has been established, staff in all areas should be notified in advance when their department will be photographed and, if possible, reminded the day before. This will give the primpers an opportunity to look their best.

There will probably be some staff members who, for whatever reason, will not want their picture taken for inclusion in the staff photo album. Aside from gently encouraging them to participate, there is little else that can be done. Reluctant staff should not (and with some, probably cannot) be forced to have their picture taken. In these cases, leave them out, but incorporate into one of the captions for their department's section of the album a note stating the conventional, "Not pictured: Jane Doe . . . "

Composing and taking the shots: With the exception of perhaps a single group shot of all or most staff in a department, formal group shots should be kept to a minimum. Informal shots of staff members at their desks or engaging in some work activity are usually more interesting. Limit the number of people per shot to two or three; otherwise, you increase unnecessarily the risk of making the picture out-of-date when someone leaves the staff. The majority of pictures should be mid-shots or close-ups since new staff members viewing the album need to be able to clearly recognize who's who. Long shots are appropriate for some group shots or, if album space permits, the department or physical area if it is being featured.

Labels and captions: A header in large type should clearly identify the department/unit being covered on the page. If space permits, a brief statement about the department's location and function could be included. Standard conventions for identifying persons in the shot should be used (e.g., Standing, l to r . . . or Back row, l to r, etc.). Again, humorous captions for some photos (particularly those shots that did not turn out exactly as planned) can lighten the tone of the album.

Making the album available: The completed photo album(s) can be made available to staff in several different ways. One or more copies could be kept by the NEO coordinator for distribution to a new employee during one of their initial meetings. At ISU, two copies of the album are on permanent reserve at the main checkout desk. This makes the album available to anyone during all hours the library is open. Circulation is limited to three days but is renewable. Another way of making the album available is to place a copy in the library staff lounge. An advantage to this arrangement over the reserve desk option is that in the lounge the album is available to all staff for casual scanning; at the reserve desk a staff member's request to see the album has to be deliberate. On the other hand, a possible disadvantage for having the album in the staff lounge is that it could leave the lounge and be temporarily (or permanently) "lost."

FACILITIES TOURS

Chances are that the interview process for a job candidate included some form of facilities tour, at least of the general area in which he or she might work. However, after officially joining the library staff, a new employee needs to be given a more in-depth orientation to the entire library facility. Who should conduct the tour is less important than making sure that appropriate touring takes place within a reasonable timeframe. At ISU, touring of the physical facility is usually handled by the mentor assigned to the new employee; however, the NEO coordinator and immediate supervisors have shared in this responsibility as well. Prior to touring the library facility, the NEO coordinator, mentor, or immediate supervisor should review the library's organizational chart to give the new employee a general idea about the library's overall administrative structure. This should help the new employee begin to develop an understanding of the various reporting relationships within and between the areas that will be visited during the tour. In addition to reviewing the organizational chart, detailed floor plans could be developed for use in the NEO program as an adjunct to the physical tour of the facility. These floor plans would be a variation of the type often provided by libraries for patrons.

In floor plans designed for library patrons, emphasis is on services areas, collection locations, and conveniences—e.g., photocopiers, vending machines and restrooms. While the same information should be included for new staff, floor plans designed specifically for new staff should be expanded to include behind the scenes locations not typically promoted to the library public, e.g., private offices, supply storage areas, and staff lounge.

The nature of a new employee's position will determine which areas of the library facility need to be visited first or emphasized the most in a tour. Obviously, initial orientation to the physical facility should focus on the new employee's immediate work area and

> Prior to touring . . . . . [the new employee should] review the library's organizational chart to give the new employee a general idea about the library's overall administrative structure. This should help the new employee begin to develop an understanding of the various reporting relationships within and between the areas that will be visited during the tour.

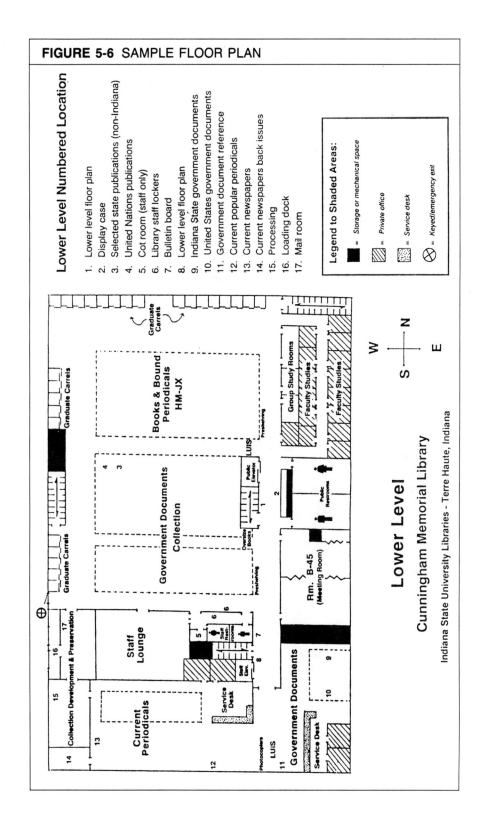

FIGURE 5-6 SAMPLE FLOOR PLAN

Lower Level Numbered Location

1. Lower level floor plan
2. Display case
3. Selected state publications (non-Indiana)
4. United Nations publications
5. Cot room (staff only)
6. Library staff lockers
7. Bulletin board
8. Lower level floor plan
9. Indiana State government documents
10. United States government documents
11. Government document reference
12. Current popular periodicals
13. Current newspapers
14. Current newspapers back issues
15. Processing
16. Loading dock
17. Mail room

Legend to Shaded Areas:

■ = Storage or mechanical space

▨ = Private office

▧ = Service desk

⊗ = Keyed/emergency exit

Lower Level

Cunningham Memorial Library

Indiana State University Libraries - Terre Haute, Indiana

department as well as convenience facilities such as restrooms, water fountains, and staff lounge. After an orientation to his or her own department, if a new employee's position requires frequent interaction with one or two other library departments or units, those areas might be logical choices for visiting first. Visits to other library departments that work closely with the new employee's department can be used to reinforce the workflow and work relationships between the new employee's unit and other library departments. Emphasizing these kinds of points during the tour should help the new employee as he or she is trying to focus on the precise role of his or her new job. The mentor, or whoever will be conducting the tour, should always contact the supervisors of the areas to be toured in advance of the visit. The tour conductor should try to schedule the visit at a time when the supervisor of the area is available to participate in the tour. This allows for a personal introduction of the new employee to the supervisor and provides a little more substance and personalization of the tour since the supervisor can make his or her own comments about the area and the relationship between that area and the new employee's department. Another important reason for actively involving the supervisor of the area is to let the new employee know who is in charge of the area, thereby reinforcing the information about lines of reporting introduced earlier during the review of the library's organizational chart.

During visits to other departments the tour conductor should take advantage of the opportunity personally to introduce the new employee to staff members in the areas visited. In advance of these introductions, the tour conductor might want to encourage the new employee to review the staff photo album before the tour to familiarize himself or herself with the people who will be met during the visit. The supervisor of the area visited can also assist with introductions, thus relieving the mentor of any possible embarrassment should he or she not know or not be able to quickly recall the names of every single person working in that area.

The overall size of the library facility will determine whether touring can be accomplished in one session. For larger library systems, several mini-tours over several days or weeks are advised. For small- and medium-sized libraries with only one main building, the tour may be handled one floor at a time. Or, as noted above, the order of visits to other departments, particularly in very large library systems, could be based on the new employee's job responsibilities as they relate to other library departments.

Some consideration should be given to the new employee's prefer-

> Visits to other library departments that work closely with the new employee's department can be used to reinforce the workflow and work relationships between the new employee's unit and other library departments.

ence for when he or she wants to begin touring outside of his or her regular work area. Interestingly enough, at ISU there have been very different preferences on the part of new employees who have gone through the NEO program as to when they want to get the "grand tour." About half have preferred to get a complete tour of the entire library facility within the first week or two of their employment. These tours are usually broken down into two or three parts. The other half of new staff has preferred to wait several weeks before getting an in-depth tour. The reason given by these new hires has been that they believe they will be able to remember more of the tour once they have digested the information about their specific job. The NEO coordinator and mentor should remember that, in addition to participating in NEO activities and receiving NEO materials, the new employee is actively engaged in job-specific training. Therefore, information overload is more of a reality than a mere possibility. If possible, the new employee should be accommodated if he or she prefers getting the library tour after he or she feels better grounded in the job.

The materials and activities presented and discussed in this chapter are those considered to be of most value to any new staff member, regardless of classification or years of experience. They should be included in starting up a new employee orientation program; however, there are numerous other materials, activities, and variations on these basics that could be either incorporated into a new program or introduced after the program has become established. In the following chapter, additional materials and follow-up activities for new employees are presented as options for inclusion in an NEO program.

The NEO coordinator and mentor should remember that in addition to participating in NEO activities and receiving NEO materials, the new employee is actively engaged in job-specific training. Therefore, information overload is more of a reality than a mere possibility.

6 ADDITIONAL MATERIALS AND FOLLOW-UP ACTIVITIES

In addition to the core materials and activities recommended in the previous chapter, there are several other simple activities that can be incorporated into an NEO program on an optional basis. Some of these might be added after a basic program has been in effect over a couple of years. Several of the recommendations that follow have not actually been put into practice at ISU, primarily because of limited time. Some of these optional activities have come about as a result of our NEO experience and observations at ISU, and some were identified in the initial review of the business literature when the NEO concept was originally researched. Each of the following suggestions offers positive benefits for a minimal investment of time and expense.

PROJECT SYNOPSES

At any given time, libraries of all types usually have one or more *major* projects or system enhancements in the planning stages or fully under way. Use of the word major in this context refers to those projects that would tend to have a significant impact, either long or short term, on some current or future library service or procedure. An extreme example would be the transition from a traditional card catalog or print index to an online public access catalog or CD-ROM network. No one on a library staff is unaffected by such changes; the impacts are systemwide and certainly significant. On the other hand, some major projects' impacts may be directed more to a particular library division, department, or unit. For example, implementation of FAX machines into a library's interlibrary loan operation has the most direct impact on the staff in that area. Likewise, implementation of an automated acquisitions process would primarily impact the acquisitions department staff. Regardless of how far-reaching the impact of a particular project or enhancement on services or procedures, all or some portion of a library's staff will be affected in some way. After all, they are the ones providing the front-line services and carrying out the day-to-day procedures.

So how should such projects be presented to a brand new employee? One approach to bringing a new employee up to speed on special projects of direct relevance to his or her particular job responsibilities is to assemble a project file for each project. A project file would include all documentation related to the project, including copies of formal communications, timelines, and program/ design specifications. But the problem with the project file approach as just described is that it will almost certainly add to the new employee's potential problem of information overload— something that should be avoided if at all possible.

While it may well be necessary for the new employee to read detailed project materials at some point soon after his or her arrival on the job, the new employee would probably appreciate it if the most important facts and data about a project were pre-identified and presented first in some coherent, summarized format. The use of project synopses or summaries is a fairly simple method of communicating a major project. A synopsis provides the employee with only the most basic project information without unduly burdening the new hire with too much detail. Project synopses have been used successfully in some business orientation programs for new employees. After studying a well-written project synopsis, an employee should have a clear, overall understanding of a project and how it affects (or will affect) his or her job and other library departments. Later, a more complete project file like the one described earlier could be provided the new employee. The more complete file would further the new employee's understanding of the project's current status by offering more details.

Project synopses should follow a standard format in terms of general layout and type of information provided. The sample project synopsis shown includes several obvious sections—"Project Title" and "Project Summary." While the summary section could include an overview of the project, the information would be broken down into parts to make the synopsis easier to scan. For example, such labels as "Impact" and "Timeline" would call immediate attention to these aspects of the project and ensure an accurate interpretation of how and when the project would affect the new employee on the job. Two other important items of information that should be broken out in the synopsis are "Local

The use of project synopses or summaries is a fairly simple method of highlighting a major project. A project synopsis provides the new employee with only the most basic project information without unduly burdening him or her with too much detail.

FIGURE 6-1 PROJECT SYNOPSIS

PROJECT SYNOPSIS
Indiana State University Libraries
Date: October 1993

Project Title: Development of an ISU Library Gopher (Internet)

Project Summary: ISU Libraries is developing a gopher server that will show up on the root menu of the University gopher as "ISU Library Gopher." The Dean of Library Services has charged a three person team to coordinate this effort. The purpose of the gopher will be to identify, organize, and provide access for library users to numerous Internet resources. The purpose of the ISU Library gopher is not to replace the existing University gopher server, but rather to focus on materials appropriate for an "electronic library."

Timeline: Development/de-bugging of non-public testbed, October through November 1993. Public Access, on or before December 1, 1993.

Impact: Initial and continuing impacts may be categorized into five broad areas--

Library Staff Training– Basic training for staff will be necessary *prior* to making the library gopher available to the public. Training is particularly important for staff who work at a public service desk, since gopher will be promoted as an electronic reference/research tool. Given the evolving nature of the Internet and its applications, staff training will most likely be an on-going issue.

Publicity– Implementation of gopher will be publicized in traditional ways: bookmarks distributed at service desks prior to public availability; articles in student/faculty publications prior to and after public access; flyers posted in various campus locations announcing ISU Libraries' gopher; instructional handouts available on the main lobby Information Rack.

End-user (public) Training and Instructional Support– Gopher concepts will be incorporated into existing library instruction activities and materials as appropriate. This will include basic coverage in selected undergraduate and graduate instructional sessions and individualized instructional sessions upon request. Special workshops offered at various times are also being considered as another option for promoting gopher and providing initial end-user training.

Collection Development Applications– The Internet is a rich information resource. Subject specialists involved in collection development will need to incorporate Internet searching into regular collection development routines. Subject specialists will be relied upon to identify new Internet resources and recommend them for addition to the ISU Library gopher.

On-going Maintenance– While initial gopher set-up is being coordinated by a three person team (see *Local Resource Persons*, below), gopher will be continuing to develop with the addition of new "connections" as they are identified by subject specialists and others. It is anticipated that the future maintenance of gopher can be handled by a graduate student under the supervision of the EIS Coordinator.

Local Resource Persons: Ralph Gabbard, Electronic Information Services Coordinator (ext. 2580; e-mail libgabb); Scott Davis, Head, Instruction & Orientation (ext. 2604; e-mail libdavi); Tom Robertson, Research Associate, Library Systems and Automation (ext. 2057, e-mail libtbr)

Additional Supporting Document(s): Contact a resource person. In addition to internal documents (Dean's charge, minutes, etc.) numerous articles and materials about the Internet, and specifically gopher, are available. Depending on your current level of Internet use, a resource person can recommend appropriate background reading.

This synopsis prepared by Scott Davis, Head, Instruction & Orientation   Date: October 15, 1993

Resource Person(s)" and "Supporting Documentation." This information would enable the new employee to seek additional information as needed.

Which new employees receive which project synopses will depend upon their particular position and the impact of any given project on their work unit. When should project descriptions be given to a new employee? Again, this will vary depending upon the immediacy of a project's impact and also on the individual's position. Synopses of projects that are imminent or already well under way, that the new employee is likely to hear about from day one, should probably be included in their welcome packet. Other synopses about projects determined not to be of immediate importance could follow after the first few days or weeks on the job.

The key to the successful use of project synopses is very similar to the points covered earlier about developing a glossary of terms and abbreviations:

1. Be selective about the projects for which you develop synopses;
2. Keep synopses simple in terms of terminology, level of detail, and layout;
3. Keep synopses brief but up-to-date;
4. Let local experts draft the synopses using guidelines similar to those suggested for glossary entries (*see* Chapter 5).

EXTENDED VISITS TO OTHER LIBRARY DEPARTMENTS

As a followup to the general tour of the library facility discussed in Chapter 5, another activity that might be desirable for some new library employees would be extended visits to certain departments, particularly those that are either directly or indirectly related in some way to the new employee's job function. What is meant by extended visit is that the new employee, rather than just take tours of the physical layouts of other library departments or units, would spend several hours to a half day or more in certain areas, observing and learning in more detail how and why things are done, general workflow, what services are provided, etc. Unless the nature of the new employee's position requires otherwise, extended visits to other library departments should probably be scheduled after the third or fourth week. An obvious exception to this recommendation would be in the orientation of a new upper-level administrator who manages several departments or units. During the first week on the job, a new administrator may want, and need, to begin spending time in the various areas he or she will be administering. As has been mentioned previously, a primary factor to remember and take into consideration about extended visits to other units and other such activities is the need to avoid prematurely overloading the new hire with information that could wait until later in the orientation process.

The value to a new employee of extended visits to other library departments should be discussed by the NEO coordinator and new employee's immediate supervisor during their initial meetings when the orientation schedule is being set.

If it is decided that such visits are worthwhile, after identifying those departments appropriate for extended visits, the NEO coordinator should contact the department heads and supervisors of those areas to coordinate visits to each area. The NEO coordinator should be prepared to assist department heads and supervisors in identifying the appropriate content to be covered during the extended visits. Ideally, the new employee should be paired with the area's supervisor, the department head, or a senior staff member in the area who is able to provide an administrator's perspective of the area's operations.

Ideally, the new employee should be paired with the area's supervisor, department head, or senior staff member in the area who would be able to provide an administrative perspective of the area's operations.

MISCELLANEOUS OTHER ACTIVITIES AND MATERIALS

Anniversary recognition: Besides posting on his or her calendar the various dates and deadlines associated with the three-month orientation period of a new hire, the NEO coordinator may want to look ahead to the first-year anniversary of the new employee and make a note. The next year, as the anniversary date approaches, the NEO coordinator might send a card, make a personal phone call, or invite the new employee for coffee during break in recognition of the employee having completed the first year on the job. The NEO coordinator might also want to contact the new employee's mentor and supervisor and remind them of the upcoming anniversary so they may participate in the recognition of the occasion as well.

Welcome banners: The market is now full of fairly inexpensive printing software that allows you to create computer banners very quickly and at practically no expense. Most of these programs have several font and graphics options. A welcome banner hung or posted in a new employee's work area on his or her first day of work, perhaps signed with personalized greetings from co-workers, would be a nice welcoming surprise for anyone.

Year-end recognition of NEO participants: At the end of the fiscal year, the NEO coordinator could compile a list of all those who have joined the staff during the year. Collective recognition of these individuals could be accomplished by publishing a brief article about NEO activities and participants in an internal staff publication, or acknowledgement could be through an announcement at an end-of-year staff meeting. While recognizing the new employees, the NEO coordinator should acknowledge library staff members who served as mentors and supervisors who participated in the NEO process.

Letters of appreciation for mentors: All activities so far have focused on the new employee. However, the mentoring process does involve the giving of time above-and-beyond the call of duty. Upon completion of a three-month NEO process, the staff member who served as mentor should receive a formal letter of appreciation from the NEO coordinator (this assumes, of course, that the person performed his or her duties well). This letter should be copied to the mentor's immediate supervisor and also to the office which maintains personnel files for all library staff. A personnel file copy serves as a good reminder of the individual's participation in this important program when it comes time for his or her next performance evaluation.

> Since the mentoring process does involve the giving of time above-and-beyond the call of duty, after completion of an NEO process for a new employee, the mentor should be sent a formal letter of appreciation.

"Mentor of the Year": Special recognition of an outstanding NEO mentor might be something to consider in large libraries with fairly high annual turnover. Recognition could come in the form of a simple announcement, a special letter of appreciation from a high-level administrator, a gift certificate, or perhaps a plaque on which is engraved the mentor's name. Recognition like this can only serve to boost morale and motivate other staff to become involved in mentoring.

Recognition upon retirement: When an NEO program has been in existence for several years, it is possible that someone who went through the program early on will retire or relocate. Depending on the circumstances of the person's departure, an NEO coordinator may want to do something special to recognize the person leaving. Since the NEO program ushered the individual into the library organization, starting a very positive work experience, there seems to be a certain symmetry to the NEO program ushering the person out on a positive note as well. Just recently at ISU, Mrs. Dee King, the first staff member to go through the NEO program, retired. Dee was in her late 50's when she joined the library staff several years ago. She is a delightful lady, and I include her in those "close work relationships" I mentioned in Chapter 3 as one of my rewards as an NEO coordinator. It occurred to me a day or two after Dee's last day at work that I really should have done something special for her—send a card, phone her, or take her for coffee, to say good-bye and to wish her well in her retirement. That hindsight is why this recommendation is made here.

Special Promotion of the NEO Program: While the positive aspects of the NEO program will do much to promote the program, another good public relations strategy would be for an NEO coordinator to solicit annually (or more or less frequently) brief written testimonials from former participants in the NEO process. This could, of course, include a former new employee (who now claims veteran status), a mentor, an immediate supervisor, even a past NEO coordinator. Each of these individuals could be asked to comment briefly on the benefits of their participation in the program. These comments could then be published in an appropriate internal staff publication. A variation of this suggestion would be to publish anonymously excerpts from the comment sections of past participants' evaluations of their NEO experience (*see* Chapter 8).

Like some of the previous suggestions, such as "Mentor of the Year" awards and letters of appreciation to mentors, any activities that serve to emphasize the positive aspects of the program can only serve to boost staff morale generally and, it is hoped, cause some staff to think, "Gee, I work in a great place!"

REGARDING SPECIALLY-PRODUCED VS. COMMERCIALLY-PRODUCED MEDIA

In the preceding discussions about NEO support materials and activities, fairly specific recommendations have been made about how information should be presented to new employees and to other NEO participants, e.g. mentor training workshops. Examples of support materials such as the staff photo album and specialized glossary are two good examples of presentation formats that are fairly easily produced and maintained in-house without a tremendous amount of expertise or creativity, or a huge amount of initial and recurring production time and expense. In the case of the instructional materials and methods recommended for the mentor training workshops, the examples tended to be equally as simple and practical, i.e., printed handouts and overhead transparencies. Obviously, there are far more sophisticated media and methods that could be incorporated into the design, development, and implementation of an NEO program. For example, computerized slide shows (instead of the more traditional 2″ × 2″ slide presentations) are becoming more commonplace; however, for such presentations to be possible and effective, one obviously has to have the necessary software and hardware and the time for planning and production.

Another high-tech instructional approach that over the past few years has received, and continues to receive, considerable attention is hypermedia/hypertext. An excellent example of a hypertext instructional application can be found at the University of Tennessee (UT). The UT library system developed a wonderful, elaborate hypertext instructional series, "New Horizons in Library Training: Computer-based Training for Library Staff," with funding from a Title II-D Department of Education Grant and also from the Apple Corporation. After reviewing this hypertext approach to library staff training, there was absolutely no doubt in my mind as to its appropriateness and desirability for an NEO program. But developing and maintaining such programs are money- and labor- intensive, and simply may not be practical or cost-effective for the medium-sized or smaller library. Larger libraries like UT often have greater access to financial and production resources. Also, they are more likely to have considerably higher staff turnover and, therefore, can better justify the investment of time and dollars for developing high-tech instructional programs. Hopefully, over the next few years as more models like these are produced, and as the technology continues to become more affordable, their use will come within reach of medium-sized and smaller libraries, not only for staff training applications, but also for patron instruction.

Other sophisticated nonprint media, though certainly more traditional than hypertext and hypermedia, include video- and audiotapes and slide (the 2″ × 2″ type) presentations. No doubt each of these media has advantages to offer in spiffing up content for presentation. Unfortunately, however, many people tend to have an automatic knee-jerk preference for the fancier media, often without seriously considering such very important factors as appropriateness, costs (in terms of both production time and money), and maintenance (updating materials as it becomes necessary). It would be hard not to argue that a multi-branched, programmed instruction hypermedia module for orienting new employees would be nice—it would. However, what would be nice and what is realistic in terms of time and resources (not only for production but also for maintenance) are almost always two different things. One should also remember the earlier acknowledgement in the Introduction of the rapid rate of technological change so prevalent in libraries today. If an instructional designer is not careful in considering the appropriateness of a particular medium (for example, hypertext or video) to the content to be presented (for example, the library's online catalog), many production hours can be spent only to have a final product that does not reflect the *major* change in the catalog that was implemented yesterday or last week!

In addition to media produced in-house, there are some commercially produced media that could be appropriate to the NEO concept and should at least be mentioned. There are several commercially produced videotapes for new employees on interacting with co-workers and the immediate supervisor. Viewing times for such tapes run anywhere from ten minutes to thirty minutes. A common problem with these commercially produced materials is that they are too general (i.e., not tailored to reflect the particulars of your library) and consequently may be ineffective at a local level. Also, costs for preview, rental, and lease/purchase tend to run very high, at least in terms of what is likely affordable for the medium-sized to small library. And, obviously, if something in one of these videotapes becomes out-of-date, the videotape becomes useless. Finally, most (if not all) of what is available commercially relates to orienting new employees in the corporate world.

7 OVERVIEW OF EVALUATION METHODS

Chapter 3 began with the acknowledgement that there is no such thing as the perfect program. A corollary to this acknowledgment would be that within any program there is always room for improvement. Just as contingency planning has been pointed to as a distinguishing mark of any good program, perhaps an even more important mark of a strong, well-developed program is the means within for systematic observation and measurement of program outcomes—i.e., evaluation. Whereas a program without a contingency planning component could probably survive by using a crisis management approach to deal with problems as they arise, a program without a systematic plan for evaluation cannot, over the long run, be realistically considered valid, promotable, or supportable from a management perspective. How could any program or service be considered legitimate if no one has bothered to substantiate to what extent program goals and objectives are met? The critical word in the preceding question is substantiate. It is one thing to *think* or *feel* that a program or service is good or operating at greatest efficiency. It is quite another to be able to base such feelings on quantitative data about the program's impact. And at a time when organizational downsizing, regardless of size, has pretty much become standard practice in management, the programs, procedures, and/or services that usually wind up first on the chopping block, and probably should, are those that cannot readily demonstrate their value to the organization's overall mission.

In philosophical debate, few library professionals would argue against the importance of program evaluation—it's a hard theoretical concept not to support. Unfortunately, however, all too often the heart of the concept is severely compromised in the course of putting theory into practice. One would be surprised at the number of libraries that lack systematic evaluation procedures for many of their services and programs, and that, even worse, pay lip service to the concept of evaluation by collecting totally irrelevant data or collecting appropriate data but never following through with the analysis. Without data analysis, identifying program weaknesses is impossible or haphazard at best, and implementing program

... a program without a systematic plan for evaluation cannot, over the long run, be realistically considered valid, promotable, or supportable from a management perspective.

... the programs, procedures, and/or services that usually wind up first on the chopping block, and probably should, are those that cannot readily demonstrate their value to the organization's overall mission.

changes toward improvement or more efficient management usually does not happen.

If evaluation is so readily recognized as an important concept, why then is it a problem in practice? The root of the problem with program and service evaluation in libraries probably lies in several different places. Do administration and research methods courses in library education programs *emphasize* evaluation and measurement? For those with professional library degrees, particularly degrees that are ten years old or older, reflect back on your graduate education. Was evaluation as a major administrative concept *and practice* given more than theoretical treatment? While library educators may be teaching the importance of evaluation, are they teaching *how* to conduct an effective evaluation and what to do with the results? Other possible reasons for weak or nonexistent program evaluation procedures are the familiar rationales "There is not enough time" and "It's *obvious* that [the program/service] is successful and operating optimally." But, if there is not enough time to evaluate a program, an administrator might logically begin to wonder if sufficient time is, in fact, being devoted to the program itself? Further, if time is such a valuable commodity (and when and where isn't it?), an administrator might ask whether a program or service is worth the time that is being devoted to it. A program's worth can only be determined through some form of systematic analysis.

And regarding the second excuse, what's obvious or held dear by those closest to a project, program, or service (i.e., the pet project), may be anything but obvious to the administrator faced with having to make service cuts in light of the big picture.

Depending on an organization's top administrative style or philosophy, it is possible that implementation of systematic evaluation procedures for generating quantitative data about programs and services may not be required or expected of middle management. This may be particularly true in small- and medium-sized organizations where administrators' do not want to be bothered with detailed evaluation data. Instead, they depend on their managers to be aware of problems, leaving it up to the individual managers to devise whatever methods they like for determining how well things are running. These administrators generally prefer to be involved in getting evaluation details only if some problem is foreseen or actually arises. So long as everything is running smoothly, they see no need to do anything about evaluations. However, sloppy management situations such as these can prove

Library educators may be teaching the importance of evaluation, a discussion that may not go beyond a statement or two, but are they teaching how to conduct an effective evaluation and what to do with the results?

disastrous to top administration and middle management when a serious problem does arise.

Frequently, the administrator who prefers to be uninvolved assumes that his or her managers are inherently capable of objectively evaluating their own operations and do such objective evaluations on some regular basis. Unfortunately, situations wherein front-line managers are given too much flexibility in determining evaluation procedures, put many of them in a position where it is very easy only to pay lip service to the concept or avoid it altogether. Many people are afraid of evaluation, perceiving it as a negative, destructive activity since it seemingly invites criticism and intervention. What these individuals fail to understand, however, is that the opposite is also true.

Evaluation provides an opportunity for recognition and reward for a job well done and can be one of the best first lines of defense for preserving good programs during times when program cuts are inevitable. But, evaluations as a management concept have received a bad rap due to an unfortunate abundance of sloppy administrators who are inept at carrying out the process.

Evaluation is good. Where the process frequently crumbles is after the evaluation when management overreacts to the evaluation results. Evaluation paranoiacs may well be justified in their attitudes about evaluation if they have had one or more bad evaluation experiences.

All levels of management have an inherent responsibility to encourage, promote, and require program and service evaluations, emphasizing their positive, constructive value in improving the organization and those in it. In communicating this, administrators have to remember that actions speak louder than words. Good programs and good performance must be overtly recognized and rewarded. But more importantly problems identified through evaluation must be addressed *positively* and *constructively;* otherwise, the positive nature of evaluations will undoubtedly be viewed as administrative lip service.

Regardless of what is *required* (or not) by high-level management, a truly competent middle manager or program coordinator will self-initiate some form of evaluation procedure that generates legitimate, worthwhile cumulative data about the area for which he or she is responsible.

This chapter is designed to address the general concept of program evaluation from a practical standpoint, as opposed to a purely theoretical one. Chapter 8 offers a practical application of program evaluation to the NEO program concept.

. . . evaluation as a management concept has received a bad rap due to an unfortunate abundance of sloppy administrators inept at carrying out the process.

FORMATIVE EVALUATION V. SUMMATIVE EVALUATION

Generally, there are two major categories of evaluation: formative and summative. Within each of these categories there are several evaluation techniques varying in degree of formality. Each technique offers its own set of advantages and disadvantages from the standpoint of how easily it can be executed and the relative quality or value of the information it yields. Further, most evaluation techniques can be either formative or summative, depending on when and how they are administered. While any single evaluation technique is better than none at all, the best option is a combination of evaluation techniques, both formative and summative, formal and informal.

Formative evaluation involves actively collecting relevant input/feedback during the course of an activity or a program. By its very nature, formative evaluation is interactive to the extent that it allows a program coordinator or service provider to adjust a program or service already in progress in an effort to maximize achievement of goals and objectives. A classic illustration of formative evaluation that most of us can identify with is the mid-term exam. The cumulative results of a class's performance on a mid-term provide the instructor with a gauge of his or her effectiveness in communicating course content in a meaningful way—i.e., teaching. Upon grading the exams and computing class averages, the instructor might determine that a majority of students are on target, mastering content at an acceptable level (C or better), and that no major changes need be made in the way the class is being taught. Likewise, an individual student's test score allows the student to gauge performance in terms of what he or she is contributing to the teaching/learning process. It may be decided that more studying is in order, fewer classes should be cut in the future, or the course should be dropped!

Formative evaluation techniques may include any of the following, so long as they are carried out one or more times prior to completion of a program or service: written evaluation instruments, direct observation, personal interviews, pre-/intermediate-/post-program measurements, self-evaluation, peer review, and focus groups. Of these evaluation techniques, the more formal ones are those that generally require more than just a little bit of time to

By its very nature, formative evaluation is "interactive". . . .

plan, execute, and analyze results. These include administering written evaluation instruments, taking pre-/intermediate-/post-program measurements, and sponsoring focus groups (*see* Chapter 1). The others can vary in their degree of formality, depending on how intricately they are planned and executed, and in how their results are analyzed. For example, an impromptu personal interview with a couple of recipients of a service or participants in a program, conducted by a service provider or program coordinator, would be considered informal if the interactions were brief and unscheduled and did not involve detailed recording of responses or comments. Another illustration of the preceding example would be the "person on the street interview" popularized years ago in radio and television advertising. On the other hand, a personal interview could be formalized to an extreme by developing a list of pre-arranged interview questions to be asked of program participants, scheduling a specific block of time for the interviews, and recording detailed information about participants' responses so they could be statistically examined for significant response trends. Depending on the statistical significance of any trends noted, conclusions could be drawn regarding the merits of a service or the effectiveness of a program. Obviously, the impromptu interview is more easily accomplished; however, the more formally developed interviews would be considered more rigorous and credible from a research standpoint, and would provide more reliable and meaningful evaluation information. In short, informal evaluation techniques are easier, but the more formal techniques provide better data.

. . . informal evaluation techniques are easier, but the more formal techniques provide better data.

Summative evaluation involves actively collecting input/feedback *ex post facto,* i.e., after the completion of a program or a service has been offered. All of the techniques identified in the previous discussion of formative evaluation could be considered summative if administered after the completion of a program or service. Summative approaches to evaluation, particularly when they are the only methods used, generally are not considered as desirable as formative approaches, or a combination of both formative and summative approaches. Since summative evaluations do not allow for direct intervention, or making corrections or adjustments to a program midstream, problems or flaws are left unaddressed until the program or service is repeated. There is no opportunity to remedy any of the problems or dissatisfactions experienced by the clients or participants involved in the first round of the program or service.

STAGES OF EVALUATION

Regardless of administrative level (whether CEO or dean, department head or program coordinator), evaluation as a basic management practice can be viewed as a three-phase process. Each phase requires conscious consideration of several questions, factors, and/or principles. The first two phases, development and implementation, are discussed below. The third phase, post-administration/followup, is the primary focus of Chapter 9.

DEVELOPMENT PHASE

This is the first phase of the evaluation process and focuses on certain theoretical questions and issues that must be considered before proceeding. Decisions made during this phase will significantly affect, either positively or negatively, the ultimate credibility of the overall process. In order to ensure an effective evaluation process, specific consideration should be given to the following areas:

> Decisions made during [the development] phase will significantly affect, either positively or negatively, the ultimate credibility of the overall process.

1. A systematic evaluation strategy/plan should be developed, even if it is not required by the administration, i.e., self-initiate the process. While today's administration may not require or desire rigorous, detailed evaluation data, tomorrow's administration might.

2. Program goals and objectives must be clearly articulated and understood. An evaluation process has no clear direction or purpose unless it is correlated to clearly stated goals. Careful attention should be given to the kinds of data that need to be collected in the evaluation process to answer questions about attainment of each and every stated goal. An evaluation effort is seriously flawed if it does not provide sufficient quantitative and/or qualitative data to answer questions about goal achievement.

3. Any evaluation method(s) is better than none at all; however, the best programs include a combination of both formative and summative and formal and informal evaluation techniques. Decide on what method or methods are best suited to the situation and begin developing prototypes. Since evaluation instruments are, in fact, surveys designed to measure outcomes, affects, and/or effects, many of the tips presented in Chapter 1 about the design of survey instruments apply to the design and development

Any evaluation method(s) is better than none at all; however, the best programs include a combination of both formative and summative and formal and informal evaluation techniques.

of an evaluation instrument. A few tips about the physical layout and design of an evaluation instrument are presented below, but a review of the survey design tips in Chapter 1 may also be in order.

Evaluation Item Design: An evaluation instrument should balance open-ended questions (soliciting some type of opinion or reaction) and closed-ended questions (soliciting simple responses, e.g., yes or no or true or false). With open-ended questions, there should be ample space for responses, as well as instructions to the respondent to continue comments on the back or attach additional sheets. An "any other comments" item should always be included for those respondents who have input not covered by another evaluation item

Evaluation Length/Completion Time Required: As with a survey instrument, the briefer and easier an evaluation is to complete, the more likely there will be a good rate of return. Generally speaking, a written evaluation instrument should not take more than about ten or fifteen minutes to complete. If needed data cannot be collected within this recommended time period, the designer of the evaluation form should consider splitting the document into a Part I and a Part II. In addition, if the evaluation instrument is about an organizational program that involves employees and is administered to employees of the organization, supervisors should allow adequate time for respondents to complete the evaluation instrument without feeling rushed.

Evaluation Revision: After an extended period of time, maybe six months to a year, depending on its scope and complexity, a program is likely to be well established. As a result, certain portions of the evaluation data that have been collected up to that point will become predictable. In such cases, the person responsible for program or service evaluations should consider revising the evaluation instruments so that new data and client perspectives are gathered.

4. Field test prototypes prior to implementation. This will not only improve the clarity and readability of the final ver-

sion of an evaluation instrument but also provide an opportunity for evaluators to conduct a mock analysis of the data collected. The mock analysis will determine if the prototype is providing all the data needed to answer questions about program goals and objectives being met.

IMPLEMENTATION PHASE

During this phase, evaluation techniques are administered and data are collected. Even though field tests of evaluation instruments have hopefully improved the final instruments, there are factors during the implementation phase that need to be remembered.

> [Over time,] certain portions of the evaluation data that have been collected . . . will become predictable. In such cases, the person responsible for program or service evaluations should consider revising the evaluation instruments so that new evaluation data and client perspectives are gathered.

1. Avoid unintentional bias (verbal or written) when administering a formal evaluation instrument or when engaging in one of the less formal techniques, such as personal interviews or direct observations. Any written instructions that appear on an evaluation instrument will have been clarified during field testing to eliminate unintentional bias. However, administering such instruments to individuals usually involves some form of contact to set up the evaluation, either a brief personal conversation, a phone call to let an individual know that the evaluation instrument is being forwarded, or a cover memo that introduces the evaluation component of a program. It is very easy to come across as a "compliment seeker" when introducing and conducting an evaluation. Some people will err toward telling you what they think you want to hear rather than being honest. Regardless of the situation, whether in written instructions on a formal evaluation, or in an informal verbal request for evaluation input, the person seeking evaluation information, should acknowledge that there is no such thing as a perfect program or service and should openly encourage constructive criticism so that the service or program can be the best that it can be.

> Some people will err toward telling you what they think you want to hear rather than being honest.

2. The evaluation process for any program or service should begin as soon after implementation as possible. Naturally, when first initiating a program, there is often a period of settling into routines and procedures. During such periods, service providers and program coordinators are well aware that all aspects of what will ultimately constitute the service or program have not yet been fully implemented. In such situations, it is appropriate to delay the evalu-

ation process but not too long, until things have settled down to a closer approximation of what is planned. Otherwise, any evaluation input you receive will likely call attention to things that are in the process of being corrected or improved as the program gets started. Following a settling-in period, any completely new program or service should be evaluated in some way frequently, maybe even at every opportunity for input. Beyond the initial or pilot implementation of a program or service, how frequently evaluation data are gathered should be a function of how many opportunities there are for collecting data. For relatively small programs or services with few participants or clients, the person responsible for getting evaluations will probably want to collect some form of evaluation input from almost everyone. Where there are numerous participants or clients, evaluation can be random (perhaps every other client, or every third client can be surveyed).

3. Either in the written instructions included on the evaluation instrument or in the verbal instructions given to respondents, the person responsible for obtaining evaluation data should indicate that the evaluation instrument is by no means the only opportunity for input. Respondents should be encouraged to contact the evaluator should they have additional thoughts or comments at some later time.

The next chapter applies the practical considerations of evaluation identified and discussed here to the evaluation of a new employee orientation program in a library setting.

Following a settling-in period, any completely new program or service should be evaluated in some way frequently.

. . . how frequently evaluation data should be gathered will be a function of how many opportunities there are for collecting data.

8 PARTICIPANT INPUT

Since the NEO program is ongoing, consisting of varying numbers of new employees going through the program during a given period of time, overall program evaluation should be conducted at a logical frequency that allows enough time to collect sufficient data. At ISU, the NEO evaluation process incorporates both summative and formative and formal and informal techniques. Evaluation instruments are administered as a component of every new employee's participation in the program. Data are accumulated and then compiled on an annual basis for overall program review.

Ultimate responsibility for initiating the evaluation process and shepherding it through various phases should lie with the NEO coordinator or perhaps staff development committee, if one exists in your library. Obviously, evaluation input should be solicited from all three of the major program participants: All new employees who have gone through the program over a specified period of time, all library staff who have served as NEO mentors, and the immediate supervisors of the new employees. Evaluation instruments should be tailored to each of these participants' roles in the NEO process and should solicit their opinions and reactions about their unique involvement in the program, as well as get their critical comments about specific program materials and activities.

During all phases of evaluating an NEO program, it should be emphasized that the purpose of the evaluation process is to evaluate the NEO *program,* not the individuals involved in it. This is particularly important because, many people are personally threatened by evaluations.

Given the one-on-one nature of the program at ISU, and the relatively small annual library staff turnover, it is difficult to collect evaluation data from participants on an anonymous basis. As noted in the 1 discussion in Chapter 1 about of survey design, respondent anonymity is best. However, ISU's NEO evaluation process is not anonymous. But, this lack of evaluation anonymity has not been identified as a problem among participants. As will be seen in the evaluation instrument samples included in this chapter, the type of information requested tends not to be sensitive from the standpoint of confidentiality. However, since there is an item on each of the different evaluation instruments asking respondents to make any other comments they care to make, there is the possibility that something will be written that should be kept confidential. In order not to discourage such candid comments, each evaluation instrument includes a statementn in the opening instruc-

---

Evaluation instruments should be tailored to each of these participants' roles in the NEO process and should solicit their opinions and reactions about their unique involvement in the program, as well as get their critical comments about specific program materials and activities.

. . . the purpose of the evaluation is to evaluate the NEO program, not the individuals involved in it.

tions that the "evaluation will be shared anonymously and only with those individuals responsible for evaluating the program."

This chapter focuses on soliciting appropriate input from all NEO program participants and is generally modeled after the NEO evaluation procedures currently followed in Indiana State University Libraries.

NEW EMPLOYEES' EVALUATION INPUT

Probably the best measure of an NEO program's effectiveness lies in the input provided by the new employees who have gone through the program. Informal input from each new employee and notes about his or her participation in the program can be gathered throughout the course of the orientation period via his or her interpersonal interactions with the NEO coordinator, NEO mentor, and immediate supervisor. The checklists maintained by these three individuals (*see* Chapter 2) should include spaces for recording miscellaneous observations about contact with the new employee. Over time, this collective informal input from numerous program participants can prove invaluable in improving program content and emphases and in better understanding the various roles and relationships that exist within the program.

Formal evaluation input is gathered from each new employee through two written evaluation instruments. Using a formative evaluation approach, Evaluation I is administered by the NEO coordinator to the new employee after his or her third or fourth week on the job. The NEO coordinator should have already mentioned the evaluation components of the NEO program during his or her initial meeting with the new employee when an overview of the entire program is presented. After about three weeks, the NEO coordinator should personally deliver the first evaluation instrument or forward it in the mail to the new employee.

The NEO coordinator should be careful not to bias the new employee's evaluation of the program by coming across as a compliment seeker; candid criticism should be encouraged in order to make the NEO program better. Evaluation I is designed to gauge the new employee's general feelings about the program and the extent to which he or she believes it is contributing to his or her

> . . . collective informal input from numerous program participants can prove invaluable in terms of improving program content and emphases and in better understanding the various roles and relationships that exist within the program.

getting the library-specific information needed. Does the employee feel that the NEO program has facilitated his or her beginning to feel like a part of the staff, as opposed to still feeling like the new kid on the block?

In addition, the new employee should be asked to consider critically each of the various materials and activities (e.g., the welcome packet and tours) of the NEO program. Were certain activities or materials particularly helpful? How could the welcome packet be improved? Is too much information included in the early stages of the NEO program?

The timing of the first evaluation coincides with the belief often reported in business literature that a new employee's overall and most lasting impressions about an organization, and his or her place in it, are usually established during the first couple of weeks on the job. By administering an evaluation instrument at this time, if any problems are detected, steps can be taken to correct the problem before the new employee has internalized potentially negative attitudes or inaccurate impressions about the organization. An employee's negative attitudes or inaccurate impressions about the library can, and probably will, have a long-term adverse effect on his or her job satisfaction, motivation, work performance, and loyalty to the library as a good place to work.

The second evaluation instrument is administered to the new employee at the end of his or her formal orientation period. At ISU, the NEO program is three months long. Since this evaluation comes after the new employee's participation in the program, it is considered a summative evaluation technique.

The second evaluation is designed to solicit the new employee's overall reaction to the program and its activities and materials, and it requires the new employee to make value judgments about whether his or her participation in the program was worthwhile. Some of the items initially addressed in the first evaluation are revisited in the second evaluation. It may be that in evaluating some of the program materials and activities after the first three weeks on the job, the new employee had not yet had an opportunity to apply some of the information, or perhaps after only three weeks on the job he or she had not yet realized the value of some of the materials and activities included in the first couple of weeks of the orientation process. The second evaluation is timed so that the new employee will have had several months to digest and apply the information given early on in the program. New-employee comments on the second evaluation are more experience-based than those gathered in the first evaluation.

By administering an evaluation instrument at this time, if any problems are detected, steps can be taken to correct the problem before the new employee has internalized potentially negative attitudes or inaccurate impressions about the organization.

FIGURE 8-1 NEW EMPLOYEE EVALUATION

NEW EMPLOYEE'S EVALUATION OF THE NEO PROGRAM--Evaluation I

Name:_____ Starting Date:_____

Position:_____

Dept./Unit:_____ Date of this eval.:_____

Having just participated in the more structured portion of the Libraries' New Employee Orientation Program, your input about the program will be helpful in improving future orientations. *This evaluation will be shared anonymously and only with those individuals responsible for evaluating the program.*

Please respond to the following items. If a response to any item is one of strong agreement or disagreement, please make clarifying comments. Attach additional sheets, if needed.

1. The "Welcome Package" included too much information.

	1	2	3	4
	Strongly Agree	Agree		Strongly Disagree

Comment:_____

_____

2. The "Welcome Package" was helpful in terms of giving me a source of basic information and should be continued in future orientations.

	1	2	3	4
	Strongly Agree	Agree		Strongly Disagree

Comment:_____

_____

3. The length of the "formal" orientation session(s) was:

	1	2	3	4
	Strongly Agree	Agree		Strongly Disagree

Comment:_____

_____

4. The orientation session(s) was a worthwhile use of your time.

	1	2	3	4
	Strongly Agree	Agree		Strongly

Comment:_____

_____

--continued on back--

FIGURE 8-1 CONTINUED

5. How useful/informative have you found the "Glossary of Common Library Terms and Abbreviations" to be?

1	2	3	4
Strongly Agree	Agree		Strongly Disagree

Comment:_____

_____

6. The "Glossary of Common Library Terms and Abbreviations" contains too many entries.

1	2	3	4
Strongly Agree	Agree		Strongly Disagree

Comment:_____

_____

7. The "Glossary of Common Library Terms and Abbreviations" should be continued in future orientations.

1	2	3	4
Strongly Agree	Agree		Strongly Disagree

Comment:_____

_____

8. Having a peer-level mentor during your first few weeks on the job has been:

1	2	3	4
Strongly Agree	Agree		Strongly Disagree

Comment:_____

_____

9. What has been the **most** positive aspect of your orientation thus far?

_____

_____

10. What has been the **least** positive aspect of your orientation thus far?

_____

_____

12. Other comments about the New Employee Orientation program:

_____

_____

THANKS FOR YOUR INPUT!

Please return this completed evaluation to the NEO Coordinator as soon as possible.

The second evaluation is timed so that the new employee will have had several months to digest and apply the information given early on in the program. New-employee comments on the second evaluation are more experience-based than those gathered in the first evaluation.

SUPERVISORS' EVALUATION

Informal input about the effectiveness of the NEO program is gathered from immediate supervisors of new employees through notes made by the NEO coordinator about his or her interactions with a supervisor during the orientation process. Informal input is also gathered from the notes and observations recorded by the immediate supervisor on his or her NEO checklist.

Formal evaluation input from the immediate supervisor of a new employee is obtained from a written evaluation instrument completed by the immediate supervisor at the end of the three-month orientation period. The NEO coordinator is responsible for forwarding the supervisor's evaluation at the appropriate time. The immediate supervisor should be reminded to return his or her NEO checklist along with the completed evaluation. The immediate supervisor's evaluation instrument solicits his or her general perceptions regarding the overall effectiveness of the NEO program. Other evaluation items could address more specific aspects of the NEO program and process. For example, was the supervisor's NEO checklist helpful? Did NEO activities significantly interfere with the new employee's job-specific training? Was the supervisor kept adequately informed by the NEO coordinator throughout the program? Did the supervisor's involvement in the program require too much of his or her time? Did the NEO program lessen the supervisor's burden of orienting the new employee to certain basic library information?

MENTORS' EVALUATION

Procedures for gathering evaluative input from NEO mentors involved in the program are basically the same as those followed with the immediate supervisors. Informal notes about the new employee/mentor relationship are recorded on the NEO coordinator's and the mentor's checklist. The NEO coordinator forwards the mentor's formal evaluation instrument to the mentor near the ned of the three-month orientation period. The mentor should be encouraged to complete and return the evaluation to the NEO coordinator as soon as possible. The mentor should also be reminded to include his or her completed checklist when forwarding the completed evaluation.

FIGURE 8-2 NEW EMPLOYEE EVALUATION II

NEW EMPLOYEE'S EVALUATION OF THE NEO PROGRAM--Evaluation II

Name:_____ Starting Date:_____

Position:_____

Dept./Unit:_____ Date of this eval.:_____

This evaluation is in follow-up to the evaluation you completed several months ago in regard to your participation in the Libraries' New Employee Orientation program. Your critical input is essential to the future effectiveness of the program. As with the past NEO evaluation, *your responses will be shared anonymously and only with those individuals responsible for evaluating the NEO program.*

Recognizing that attitudes and reactions change over time, several of the evaluation items below address areas also covered on the first evaluation. Please respond to each item, and when possible, make any comments which might clarify your responses. Attach additional sheets, if needed.

1. Using the following rating scale, please indicate your overall "attitude" about/reaction to each of the following aspects of the NEO program:

    1 = Very positive/Very helpful   4 = Generally negative/generally not helpful

    2 = Generally positive/generally helpful   5 = Very negative/very unhelpful

    3 = Neither a positive or negative reaction   N/A = Not applicable

    _____ the NEO "Welcome Package"

    _____ the "Welcome Letter" you received before starting your job here

    _____ the *Glossary of Common Library Terms and Abbreviations*

    _____ the maps/floor diagrams of the library

    _____ the initial orientation session(s)

    _____ having a mentor during your first few months

    _____ the overall organization of the NEO program

    _____ the overall effectiveness of the NEO program

    _____ the library staff handbook

    _____ the staff photo album

    _____ project synopses

    _____ guided tour(s) of the library

    _____ other: (please specify)_____

    _____

--continued on back--

FIGURE 8-2 CONTINUED

2. Do you think the NEO program should be required for all new employees of the library?

_____ Yes   _____ No

Please indicate why or why not?_____

_____

_____

3. Having participated in the NEO program, might you be interested in serving as an NEO Mentor in the future? *(check your response)*

_____ Yes   _____ No   _____ Maybe

4. If the library did *not* have an orientation program for all new employees, do you think it would have made a difference in the way you feel about being a member of the library staff, or in the way you learned about the library as an organization?

_____ Yes, definitely   _____ No, probably not   _____ Maybe

5. Make at least one suggestion for improving the NEO program. *(please be specific)*

_____

_____

6. Overall, what was the **most** positive aspect of the NEO program?

_____

_____

_____

7. Overall, what was the **least** positive aspect of the NEO program?

_____

_____

_____

8. Other comments about your experiences in the NEO program:

_____

_____

_____

THANKS FOR YOUR INPUT!

Please return this completed evaluation to the NEO Coordinator as soon as possible.

FIGURE 8-3 SUPERVISOR'S EVALUATION

NEO MENTOR'S EVALUATION OF THE NEO PROGRAM

Name:_____ Date of eval.:_____

Served as NEO Mentor for:_____
(Name of new employee)

Beginning/Ending Dates of mentoring:_____

Having served as an NEO Mentor, your critical reactions and suggestions regarding your mentoring experience will be helpful in improving future orientations. *This evaluation will be shared anonymously and only with those individuals responsible for evaluating the NEO program.*

Please respond to the following. If possible, please make comments that might clarify your response. Attach additional sheets for comments, if needed.

1. Do you feel that the mentoring component of the NEO program contributes to the overall goals of the NEO program? Why or why not?

   _____

   _____

2. A mentor training workshop held prior to your serving as a mentor would have helped to clarify your duties as an NEO Mentor.

1	2	3	4
Strongly Agree	Agree		Strongly Disagree

   Comment:_____

   _____

3. Would you volunteer again to serve as a new employee's mentor?

   _____ Yes   _____ No   _____ Maybe

   If your response was "no" or "maybe," please elaborate:_____

   _____

   _____

4. Your mentoring experience, overall, required too much of your time and attention.

1	2	3	4
Strongly Agree	Agree		Strongly Disagree

   Comment:_____

   _____

5. The mentoring component of the NEO program is too structured.

1	2	3	4
Strongly Agree	Agree		Strongly Disagree

--continued on back--

FIGURE 8-3 CONTINUED

Comment regarding item #5: _____

_____

6. The mentoring process turned out to be a good learning experience for you.

1	2	3	4
Strongly Agree	Agree		Strongly Disagree

Comment: _____

_____

7. What was the **most** positive aspect of serving as an NEO mentor?

_____

_____

_____

8. What was the **least** positive aspect of serving as a mentor?

_____

_____

_____

9. Make at least one suggestion for improving the NEO program *(please be specific)*:

_____

_____

10. Other comments about your mentoring experience or the NEO program in general:

_____

_____

_____

_____

THANKS FOR YOUR INPUT!

Please return this completed evaluation to the NEO Coordinator as soon as possible.

The mentor's evaluation instrument should include questions about such aspects of the program as the effectiveness of the mentor training workshops attended before serving as a mentor; the time commitment required to serve as a mentor and effect on the supervisor's job-specific duties; the overall structure of the mentoring component of the NEO program (too structured? not structured enough?); and the extent to which communications with other program participants was adequate—i.e., whether the supervisor was kept properly informed throughout the process.

NEO COORDINATOR'S EVALUATION

The NEO coordinator serves as the initiator of the evaluation process and the collector, organizer, synthesizer, and summarizer of all the data generated by it. The regular intervals at which the overall NEO program will be evaluated will depend on the number of new employees participating in the program over a specified period of time. At ISU, the NEO program is reviewed on an annual basis.

Overall program evaluation involves compiling the evaluation data collected from all program participants over the designated period of time. A more detailed discussion of compiling evaluation data is found in the section in Chapter 9, "Deriving Meaning from Evaluation Data."

After compiling the data, the NEO coordinator should prepare an executive summary, to be forwarded to higher-level administration for review and comment. The purpose of the executive summary is to provide a brief overview that highlights major evaluation results or findings, notes program strengths and weaknesses, offers possible explanations for any unexpected findings, and poses strategies or questions about dealing with any problem areas that may have been identified through the evaluation process. The executive summary, by definition brief, should be comprehensive to the extent that it provides enough information about the program for the period being evaluated for the staff development committee or for library administration to be able to make confident recommendations about continuing the program as is or offering suggestions for improvement. Even though the executive summary

The NEO coordinator serves as the initiator of the evaluation process, and as the collector, organizer, synthesizer, and summarizer of all the data generated by it.

FIGURE 8-4 MENTOR'S EVALUATION

IMMEDIATE SUPERVISOR'S EVALUATION OF THE NEO PROGRAM

Name:_____ Date of eval.:_____

Immediate Supervisor of:_____
(Name of new employee)

Beginning/ending dates of orientation period:_____

Having just participated as an immediate supervisor in the NEO program, your critical reactions and suggestions about the program will be helpful in improving future orientations. This evaluation will be shared only with those individuals responsible for evaluating the NEO program.

Please respond to the following. If possible, please make comments that might clarify your response. Attach additional sheets, if needed.

1. Did you find the Supervisor's NEO Checklist helpful? _____ Yes _____No

   If your response was "no," please elaborate:_____

   _____

2. The NEO program was a worthwhile use of your and your new employee's time.

1	2	3	4
Strongly Agree	Agree		Strongly Disagree

   Comment:_____

   _____

3. Your participation in the NEO program required too much of your time and interfered with more pressing duties.

1	2	3	4
Strongly Agree	Agree		Strongly Disagree

   Comment:_____

   _____

4. The NEO program interfered significantly with the new employee's job-specific training.

1	2	3	4
Strongly Agree	Agree		Strongly Disagree

   Comment:_____

   _____

5. The NEO Coordinator kept you informed of activities as appropriate, was available to offer assistance when needed, and considered your suggestions in cooperative activities.

1	2	3	4
Strongly Agree	Agree		Strongly Disagree

--continued on back--

FIGURE 8-4 CONTINUED

Comments regarding item #5:_____

_____

6. The NEO program lessened your burden of orienting the new employee to certain basic information.

1	2	3	4
Strongly	Agree		Strongly
Agree			Disagree

   Comment:_____

   _____

7. From your standpoint as an immediate supervisor of a new employee, what was the **most** positive aspect of the NEO program?

   _____

   _____

   _____

8. What was the **least** positive aspect of your involvement in the NEO program?

   _____

   _____

   _____

9. Make at least one suggestion for improving the supervisor's role in the NEO program (please be specific)

   _____

   _____

   _____

10. Other comments you would about your role as immediate supervisor in the NEO program, or the program in general:

   _____

   _____

   _____

   _____

THANKS FOR YOUR INPUT!

Please return this completed evaluation to the NEO Coordinator as soon as possible.

does not include all the raw data collected by the NEO coordinator during the evaluation period, it should include a statement that all raw evaluation data are available for review by the staff development committee or administration if that is deemed necessary. In lieu of including all raw data in the executive summary, the NEO coordinator may include as an attachment or an appendix a master tally of each evaluation instrument. Each master tally would report cumulative totals to all (or major) evaluation items. Cumulative totals could be expressed as whole numbers and as percentages of the total response to an evaluation item.

REVIEW BY THE STAFF DEVELOPMENT COMMITTEE AND LIBRARY ADMINISTRATION

At ISU, the executive summary of the NEO program evaluation is forwarded to the library staff development committee and copied to the dean of library services. The organizational structure in ISU Libraries is such that the administrative charge to the staff development committee includes a specific statement regarding its role in the review and evaluation of the NEO program. The staff development committee makes recommendations to the library administration about program continuation and improvement. A cover memorandum accompanies the executive summary to the staff development committee, correlating the document to the committee's charge. The committee is invited to contact the NEO coordinator should it need clarification of any points raised in the executive summary or if it wishes to see all or a part of the raw data used to draw conclusions included in the executive summary. Finally, a statement is included in the cover memorandum expressing appreciation to the committee for its critical review of the program and requesting that the committee share with the NEO coordinator their formal administrative recommendations/comments.

In the absence of a staff development committee, the executive summary would be sent to the library administrative officer assigned responsibility for the program. Obviously, how the summary is handled beyond that point will be a function of local administrative policy, procedure, and style. The NEO coordinator should however, include the usual statement asking administration to share its reaction toward the summary, and any recommendations about how the program should be continued in the future, with the NEO coordinator.

The purpose of the executive summary is to provide a brief overview that highlights major evaluation results or findings, notes program strengths and weaknesses, and offers possible explanations for any unexpected findings.

9 UTILIZING EVALUATION RESULTS

As noted in Chapter 7, the evaluation process requires the completion of three distinct phases: development, implementation, and post-administration/follow-up. The absence of, or an indifference to any one of these phases severely compromises, if not totally negates, the effectiveness of the overall process. To gather evaluative information one has to follow the general recommendations about the development and implementation of evaluation instruments discussed in Chapter 7. But even then, all can go for naught if there is no systematic or logical approach to evaluation of the data during the third phase—post-administration followup. What is to be done with the raw evaluation data?

As easy as it would be to review casually the evaluation input and draw informal conclusions along the lines of, "Oh, that's nice," or "Ooh, they may have a point there," what's *the point* of the process if some systematic action is not taken to derive meaning from the collective evaluation input, if logical conclusions based on the collective input are not formulated, and if specific actions are not taken to react to the conclusions? The focus of this chapter is on evaluation followup, which is probably the most important of the three evaluation phases in terms of making the time spent on the process worthwhile.

While extremely sophisticated statistical analyses could be performed on the raw evaluation data, such analyses are not necessary to make some sound in-house observations and draw conclusions about the overall strengths and weaknesses of a program. This chapter offers practical suggestions and advice about this phase of the evaluation, without using the services of a major-league statistician.

The NEO evaluation process described in the two preceding chapters will result in a pile of filled-out formal evaluation instruments and informal checklist notes generated by NEO program participants. Before describing for you what an in-depth analysis of the data entails, let me share with you some conclusions of mine based on our program. First, even though significant time has been spent on trying to make the evaluation process an observable, quantifiable, and objective process, it is important to remember that it is still basically a subjective process since it relies heavily (if not exclusively) on the perceptions and recollections of program participants. However, as will be discussed shortly, the seemingly sub-

> The evaluation process requires the completion of three distinct phases: development, implementation, and post-administration followup. The absence of, or an indifference to, any one of these phases severely compromises . . . the potential effectiveness of the overall process.

. . . even though significant time has been spent on trying to make the evaluation process an observable, quantifiable, and objective process, it is still basically a subjective process since it relies heavily, if not exclusively, on the perceptions and recollections of program participants.

jective nature of evaluation data can be converted so the data can be interpreted fairly objectively.

Second, no single evaluation response or comment means anything in isolation. Remember: "The whole is greater than the sum of its parts." So evaluation data have no real meaning until they have been synthesized into something larger, i.e. the proverbial "big picture" that usually has a totally new meaning of its own. Consequently, to get the complete picture, the individual(s) responsible for evaluating the program should personally review *all* evaluative observations; every completed formal evaluation instrument and every recorded participant comment should be seen by the person responsible for the final analysis. In the course of reviewing formal observations and comments, such persons should not overreact to a single negative comment or even a relative few, but rather they should be aware of the overall frequency of negative observations. Human nature is such that we all tend to remember and, all too frequently, to internalize the negatives, regardless of how they may be outweighed by a larger number of positives. Criticisms tend to stick in our memories longer and receive more attention than they sometimes deserve, particularly in the case of unanticipated criticism. One or two blatantly negative comments from a collection of 50 observations should not be given too much attention. On the other hand, anything approaching only 75 percent positive response/agreement of all observations (i.e., 25 percent negative response/disagreement) should get the attention of the sponsor of the evaluation and should be more closely examined to determine what is going on.

. . . evaluators should not over react to single negative comments or to only a relative few. . . .

DERIVING MEANING FROM EVALUATION DATA

Data analysis begins by calculating cumulative responses to each question on each evaluation instrument. This is best accomplished by creating a master tally sheet for each different evaluation instrument used in the process. In terms of the model being presented in this manual, there would be four separate evaluation tally sheets: one for New Employee Evaluation I, one for New Employee Evaluation II, one for immediate supervisor evaluations, and one for mentor evaluations. Tally sheets would be identical to their corresponding evaluation instrument; however, there should be space between quantitative (close-ended) questions to allow sufficient room for tallying individual responses to each choice included in the question. A separate sheet should be devoted to the tallying of each qualitative question (open-ended/comments) since their tally involves compiling a verbatim list of all comments to the question. After master tally sheets are set up, each individual evaluation instrument collected during the evaluation period is posted item-by-item to the appropriate master tally; at ISU, hash marks are used to record each quantitative response. Though possibly a time-consuming process (depending on the number of new employees who participated in the program during the evaluation period), the tallying of individual evaluations can be done by a competent student assistant or library volunteer. After the posting of quantitative items is completed, totals are determined for each response option in a given question. These totals are added for each question to determine the total number of responses. Next, percentages are calculated for each of the item's response options. As an example, a close-ended quantitative evaluation question may request the respondent to check either "yes," "no," or "no opinion" as his or her response. By figuring total responses to the question and the total of each response option, the person conducting the analysis can state that "of 20 responses, 12 (60 percent) indicated 'yes,' 1 (5 percent) indicated 'no,' and 7 (35 percent) indicated they had 'no opinion'." Likert-type evaluation questions that ask respondents to rate their opinion or level of agreement on a numbered scale (e.g., 1 = strongly disagree through 4 = strongly agree) can be quantified and reported in a number of ways. First, the average response rating among all respondents to such a question can be calculated by summing the ratings to all response options and dividing by the total number of responses to the question. Second, the distribution of responses to each option can be tallied and reported as a percentage of the total number of responses to an item.

Response distributions and/or averages of Likert-type responses to each question allow those responsible for the evaluation to draw conclusions about the cumulative response to the question. These conclusions are then correlated with the appropriate program goals or objectives.

The relationship between the conclusions and the desired goals/objectives determine whether the goal/objective has been accomplished to a satisfactory level. What constitutes "satisfactory level" is a decision that has to be made locally. However, a model

. . . tallying of individual evaluations can be done by a competent student assistant or library volunteer.

that most people find meaningful is the traditional American grading scale. In the case of percentages, 100 percent would be excellent, 90 percent good, etc., all the way down to 60 percent and below which would be failing.

As mentioned, qualitative questions should be compiled into a master list. Upon completion of the list, each comment should be carefully considered by the person(s) doing the evaluation, and a general valence should be assigned to the item: + for those comments that are clearly positive or supportive, - for those that are negative or non-supportive, and ± for those comments that are neutral—i.e., are neither positive nor negative but, rather, a neutral observation. Once a valence has been assigned to each comment, the comments can be grouped and tallied to determine the positive, negative, and neutral response distribution and the percentage of each in relation to the total number of responses to each question. The same process of drawing conclusions and pairing with appropriate goals and objectives as described above is applied to qualitative questions to make judgments about goal achievement.

> Response distributions and/or averages of Likert-type responses to each question allow those responsible for the evaluations to draw conclusions about the cumulative response to the question. . . . The relationship between the conclusions and the desired goals/objectives determine whether the goal/objective has been accomplished. . . .

HAVE PROGRAM GOALS BEEN MET?

Once data have been quantified in some way, the program evaluator(s) should return to the original goals and objectives that were established at the outset of the program. If the evaluation instruments used in the process were developed so that they correlate with program goals and objectives, as recommended in Chapter 7, then there should be one or more cumulative evaluation figures that can be matched to each goal and each objective. Goals and objectives are almost always definitive statements. In trying to determine if goals and objectives of the NEO program have been met, one way to simplify the process is to convert the original goal statements into questions. For example:

> In trying to determine if goals and objectives of the NEO program have been met, one way to simplify the process is to convert the original goal statements into questions.

- Original goal: A goal of the NEO program is to make all new library employees feel welcome and comfortable as they begin their new job.
- Evaluation question: Did the NEO program help make new library employees feel welcome and comfortable as they began the new job?

Two evaluation items that are correlated to this particular program goal are included in the second new employee evaluation. They are:

- Item #2: Do you think the NEO program should be required of all new employees of the library? Yes or No. Please indicate why or why not?
- Item #4: If the library did not have an orientation program for all new employees, do you think it would have made a difference in the way you feel about being a member of the library staff, or in the way you learned about the library's organization? Response choices: Yes, definitely; no; maybe.

The cumulative responses to these two items should provide data to support a "yes" or "no" answer to the goal evaluation question. For example, cumulative data totals could be incorporated into a brief paragraph like the following:

Of 40 new library employees participating in the NEO program during the preceding year, 39 (or 97.5 percent) indicated that they thought the program should be required of all new library employees. The reasons cited by new employees for this perception included " . . . I felt like I belonged from day one," and "I never had the feeling that I wasn't immediately a part of the 'library team'." In addition, all 40 new employees were unanimous in the opinion that the NEO program definitely made a difference in the way they felt about being a member of the library staff and the way they learned about the library's organization.

The preceding process should be followed for each stated program goal and objective.

In the Introduction to this manual, it was noted that NEO program goals could be categorized into staff-specific goals (those providing direct benefits to staff members) and organization-specific goals (those providing benefits to the organization). The evaluation process described thus far has dealt with staff-specific program goals and objectives. Evaluation of organization-specific goals would be a separate process and is not treated in detail in this manual. But let me say here that the evaluation process to determine the extent to which organization-specific goals have been met would involve a longer term study than the process described for staff-specific goals. Such a study would be conducted after the NEO program had been in existence for several years. Special evaluation instruments would need to be designed for gathering information about the NEO program's relationship to such organizational factors as retention rates, employee job satisfaction, communication between employees and supervisors, and employee loyalty to the organization. In addition, the study would require fairly sophisticated analyses of organizational statistics such as job turnover, retention, etc., in order to legitimately establish any kind of cause and effect relationship between the NEO program and organization-specific goals and objectives.

ACTING ON CONCLUSIONS: INITIATING PROGRAM REVISION

The answers to goal evaluation questions will be the prime determinants of what program adjustments need to be made or considered. One particular revision that may be needed involves "tightening up" the original evaluation instruments. In the process of correlating evaluation data with goal evaluation questions, the person(s) conducting the evaluation may discover that additional items are needed on the various evaluations to better answer goal evaluation questions. Or, similarly, an evaluation question that was originally perceived to be appropriate turns out in reality to be vague or incomplete. For example, assume that the cumulative response data for one particular evaluation question is generally negative, but the question did not include an opportunity for respondents to add clarifying comments. The question clearly seems to identify a program weakness or problem, but without clarifying comments from respondents the person conducting the evaluation can only guess at possible reasons for the overall negative perception. If such is the case, that question should be reworded or expanded to provide more useful data in the future.

The need for additional program revisions or changes might also come from those open-ended evaluation questions which ask respondents to identify the most positive and least positive aspects of the program. All the variations of the evaluation instruments included a final item that invited respondents to make any comment at all about their feelings, attitude about, or experience with the NEO program. Cumulative responses to this question might result in the person(s) conducting the evaluation giving consideration to a wide range of program adjustments, from decreasing the amount of information in the welcome packet to reorganizing or adding a section to the staff handbook. Other cumulative responses may support the overall conclusion that the program is running smoothly and that all materials and activities are good just as they are, therefore, the program requires no action at all.

SHARING EVALUATION CONCLUSIONS WITH PARTICIPANTS AND LIBRARY STAFF

After the library administration has reviewed the evaluation summary described in Chapter 8, the NEO coordinator should receive some form of official acknowledgement of the administration's reaction to the summary. The acknowledgement should give a clear indication of continuing administrative support of the program or make specific recommendations for addressing any problem areas identified in the evaluation summary. Upon receiving word from the administration, the NEO coordinator or perhaps the staff development committee should take steps to share highlights of the evaluation process with the entire library staff. This could be done via a special memo sent to all library staff or by an article published in an internal staff publication. The NEO evaluation summary for staff should be relatively brief but should identify major program strengths and include any substantiating data and/or particularly well-phrased comments made on an evaluation instrument. Quotes should be cited anonymously unless the NEO coordinator has requested and received permission to identify the staff member who made the comment. In cases of positive statements, most staff members would likely be pleased to see their names in print associated with a positive, pro-NEO statement.

In addition to identifying program strengths in a report to all staff, it is equally important to identify program weaknesses that were identified during the evaluation process. Those staff members who participated in the evaluation process and offered criti-

. . . take steps to share highlights of the evaluation process with the entire library staff.

cisms will probably recall what prompted their critical responses. By seeing an acknowledgement of a weakness that they helped identify, they will likely appreciate confirmation that their comments were heard and the evaluation process really does work.

In identifying program weaknesses, care should be taken to word statements as positively as possible, particularly if the weakness is related in any way to the general roles of mentors or supervisors. Also, after a weakness has been identified, a concise statement should follow indicating what specific actions are planned or are already being taken by the NEO coordinator or library administration to address the problem in the future.

In the next cumulative evaluation process, any program weaknesses identified the year before (or at whatever regular interval is adopted for the evaluation) should be revisited, and a statement should be included indicating whether the problem was solved during the preceding year. Finally, an NEO evaluation summary for distribution to all staff should close with a statement of appreciation to all those who participated in the program and evaluation process.

Beyond sharing a summary of NEO program evaluation results with internal staff, the NEO coordinator should encourage the library administration to include specific mention of the NEO program, as might be appropriate, in annual reports, presentations to governing boards or professional organizations, and local or campus media releases. Sharing information about the positive aspects of the library's NEO program is good public relations and could help with staff recruitment. Those outside the library will see a report of a successful library NEO program as positive evidence that the library is a good place to work, where the administration cares about the staff.

> ... after a weakness has been identified, a concise statement should follow indicating what specific actions are planned by the NEO coordinator or library administration to address the problem in the future.

CONCLUSION

During the later 1980s, the need for orienting the new employees of Indiana State University Libraries in a systematic way was clearly established—library staff expressed the need during staff development activities, and an outside consultant also recommended the development of such a program. Since implementation of the new employee orientation (NEO) program, the program has proven to be not only possible within the existing organizational structure of ISU Libraries but also desirable—the professional literature of personnel management clearly supports the fact that time spent orienting new hires to the organizational culture of their new work environment is a wise investment.

The initial success and the ultimate good health of any NEO program requires at least two things. First, the library administration must commit to such a program. This commitment must come in the form of policy support, financial support, and positive acknowledgement of the activities of those people integrally involved in the program. Secondly, each library staff member, regardless of his or her position within the organization or the extent of his or her direct involvement in the NEO program, must acknowledge the fact that every staff member's job is important not only to the immediate work unit or department but to the whole library. New employees are no less important nor their potential for contributing to the organization any less—than the employee who has been on the job for 30 years. In fact, "the person who started work this morning is, at least attitudinally, as close to a 'model employee' as you'll ever get" (Posner, 1986, p. 73).

SELECTED
BIBLIOGRAPHY

———. *Developing and Improving Clients' Recruitment, Selection, and Orientation Programs*. New York: AICPA, Management Consulting Services, 1992.

———. "Staff Development" (unpublished policy statement from the Library Administration). Terre Haute, Indiana: Indiana State University Libraries, 1989.

———. "Staff Development" (unpublished report from the Task Force on the Future of Staff Development). Terre Haute, Indiana: Indiana State University Libraries, 1989.

Addams, H. Lon. "Up to Speed in 90 Days: An Orientation Plan." *Personnel Journal,* 64 (December, 1985):35-38.

Arthur, Diane. "The First Day at Work." *Management Solutions,* 31 (October, 1986): 37-42.

———. *Recruiting, Interviewing, Selecting & Orienting New Employees*. New York: AMACOM, American Management Association, 1991.

Brechlin, Jeff and Allison Rossett. "Orienting New Employees," *Training,* 28 (April 1991):45-51.

Brody, E. W. "What Do You Do With a New Employee?" *Public Relations Quarterly,* 31 (Fall, 1986):25.

Cohen, Madeline E. "Training 101: Orientation—The First Step in Team Building." *Training and Development Journal,* 42 (January, 1988):20-23.

Comer, Debra R. "Peers as Providers," *Personnel Administrator,* 34 (May 1989):84-86.

Cook, Mary F. *The AMA Handbook for Employee Recruitment and Retention*. New York: American Management Association, 1992.

Cooke, Rhonda. "Employee Orientation Helps Beat the 'First Day' Blues," *Credit Union Management,* 12 (October 1989):20-21.

Corey, Constance. "Those Precious Human Resources: Investments That Show You Care Enough to Keep the Very Best." *Library Administration & Management,* 2 (June, 1988):128-131.

Cowan, Robert A. "Welcoming New Employees," *American Printer,* 205 (May 1990):88, 90.

Davidson, Jeffrey P. "Starting the New Hire on the Right Foot." *Personnel,* 63 (August, 1986):67-71.

Day, Dave. "Training 101: A New Look at Orientation." *Training and Development Journal,* 42 (January, 1988):18-20.

Ensor, Pat, et al. "Strategic Plan for Indiana State University Libraries: 1987-1992". Terre Haute, Indiana: Indiana State University Libraries, 1987. ERIC Document 290-490.

Federico, Richard F. "Six Ways to Solve the Orientation Blues," *HR Magazine,* 36 (May 1991):69-70.

Finch, Frank. *The Facts on File Encyclopedia of Management Techniques.* New York: Facts on File Publishing, 1985.

Geromel, Gene. "A Good Start for New Hires." *Nation's Business,* 77 (January, 1989):21-22.

Jerris, Linda A. *Effective Employee Orientation.* New York: AMACOM, 1993.

Kiechel, Walter. "Love, Don't Lose, the Newly Hired." *Fortune,* 118 (June 6, 1988):271,274.

Kliem, Ralph Leonard. "Welcoming New Employees the Right Way." *Administrative Management,* 48 (July, 1987):14-15.

Klubnik, Joan P. "Orienting New Employees." *Training and Development Journal,* 41 (April, 1987):46-49.

Martin, Thomas N. and Joy Van Eck Peluchette. "Employee Orientation: Not Just for the Company's New Hires." *Personnel Administrator,* 34 (March, 1989):60,63-64.

McKenna, Joseph F. "Training: Welcome Abroad!" *Industry Week,* 238 (November 6, 1989):31-38.

Mishra, Jitendra M. and Pam Strait. "Employee Orientation: The Key to Lasting and Productive Results." *Health Care Supervisor,* 11 (March, 1993):19-29.

Nelson, Andre. "New Employee Orientations—Are They Really Worthwhile?" *Supervision,* 51 (November, 1990):6-8.

Posner, Bruce G. "The First Day on the Job." *Inc.,* 8 (June, 1986):73-75.

Ray, Darrel W. "Important Impressions: You Only Get One Chance to Influence a New Employee." *Management World,* 17 (March/April, 1988):34-35.

Reinhardt, Claudia. "Training Supervisors in First-Day Orientation Techniques." *Personnel,* 65 (June, 1988):24,26,28.

Rosenberg, Jane A. and Maureen Sullivan. *Resource Notebook on Staff Development.* Washington, D.C.: Office of Management Studies (OMS), Association of Research Libraries, 1983.

Segall, Linda J. "Integrating Your New Employee into the Organization." *Supervisory Management,* 31 (February, 1986):12-14.

Shea, Gordon F. *The New Employee: Developing a Productive Human Resource.* Reading, MA: Addison-Wesley Publishing Company, 1981.

Smith, Ronald E. "Employee Orientation: 10 Steps to Success." *Personnel Journal,* 63 (December, 1984):46-48.

Stewart, David and Prem N. Shamdasani. *Focus Groups: Theory and Practice.* Newbury Park, CA: Sage Publications, 1990.

Sullivan, Maureen. "Indiana State University [Libraries] Consultation on Staff Development" (unpublished consultant's report), 1988.

Wilkinson, Roderick. "All-Purpose Employee Handbook," *Supervision,* 53 (January, 1992):5-7.

Zemke, Ron. "Employee Orientation: A Process, Not a Program," *Training,* 26 (August 1989):33-38.

INDEX

administration, support of NEO concept by, 2, 137

benefits, neo program, viii, xi
brainstorming, 9-16
    defined, 9, 14
    facilitator, 14-15
    participant selection, 15-16
    recorder, 14-15
    results, interpretation of, 16
    rules of, 14
    topics, 15

checklists,
    as organizational tools, 26
    immediate supervisor, 30-31
    mentor, 34-35, 62-63
    neo coordinator, 27-28
    welcome packet, 75-76
clip art, 82, 84
community resources, 3
contingency planning, 37, 105
continuing education, ix

dropouts, 42-43

evaluation, 105-137
    bias, 112
    design, 111
    development phase, 110-112
    formal, 108-109
    formative, 108-109
    frequency of, 112-113
    implementation phase, 112-113
    informal, 108-109
    overview of methods, 105-113
    post-administration/follow-up phase, 115, 129
    stages/phases of, 110-113, 129
    summative, 108-109

floorplans, library, 90-91
    sample, 91
focus groups, 16-19
    defined, 16-17
    moderator, 17-18
    participants, 18
    results, interpretation of, 18-19
formative evaluation, 108-109

glossary of library terms and abbreviations, 80-85
    cover, sample, 84
    format and layout, 82
    revisions and upkeep, 85
    sample entries, 83
goals, neo program, viii-xi
group approach to orientations, 19-20

hypertext, 102

immediate supervisors, see supervisors, immediate
ineffective participants, 39-41
information overload, viii, 73, 93

job-specific training vs. orientation, 24

media,
    commercially-produced, 102-104
    slide presentations, 102, 103
    specially-produced (in-house), 102-104
mentors,
    checklist, 34-35, 62-63
    defined, 32
    duties and responsibilities, 32, 54, 61-62

evaluation form, sample, 126-127
evaluation of neo program, 64, 120, 126-127
letters of appreciation to, 100
mismatches with new employees, 45-46, 64-65
selection, 32-33, 62, 71
supervisor's approval for participation, 33, 71
time requirement, 54, 61
training workshops, 52-67
training workshops, evaluation of, 66-67
training workshops, transparency masters, 55-59
"Mentor of the Year," 100
mismatched mentors and new employees, 45-46, 64-65

name tags, library staff, 86
neo coordinator,
    as staff psychologist and personal advisor, 47-48
    checklist, 27-28
    duties and responsibilities, 24-26
    evaluation summary of neo program, 125, 128
    initial meeting with supervisor, 69-71
neo program,
    benefits, v, vii
    content, general, 20-21
    documentation, 21
    evaluation, 115-137
        interpreting results of, 129-132
    evaluation results, sharing, 135-136
    follow-up activities and materials, 95-102
    goals, v-vii

neo program, *continued*
  participants, 23-36
  problems, 37-49
    coordinator as staff
      psychologist, 47-48
    dropouts, 42-43
    ineffective participants,
      39-41
    mismatched mentors/new
      employees, 45-46, 65
    short notice of new staff
      arrival, 41-42
    staff development com-
      mittee, importance,
      48-49
    staff resistance, 43-44
  promotion, 101
  rationale and goals, v-vii,
    132-134
  revision, 134-135
  structure, 19-20
  timeline, 21
  welcome letter, 67, 69, 70
  welcome packet, 75-76
new employee,
  anniversary recognition,
    99-100
  evaluation forms, sample,
    118-119, 121-122
  evaluation of neo program,
    116-120, 121-122
  introductions to staff, 86
  job satisfaction, viii, xi
  job-specific training, ix, 6
  mismatches with mentor,
    45-46, 64-65
  productivity, viii, xi
  retirement recognition, 101

one-on-one approach to orienta-
    tions, 19-20
organizational structure, library,
    1-2
orientation vs. job-specific-
    training, 24

performance evaluation, 2, 29
personnel librarian, 2
personnel management/business,
    literature of, viii-15
photo album, staff, 86-90
  availability to staff, 89-90
  design and layout, 87-89
  upkeep, 87
problems, anticipating and
    troubleshooting, 37-49
project synopses, 95-98
  format, 96, 98
  sample, 97

short notice of new staff arrival,
    41-42
slide presentations, 102, 103
staff development, administrative
    position/support, 2, 137
staff development committee, 23,
    128
  importance of, 48-49
staff development in libraries,
    vii-viii, 2
staff handbook, library, 77-79
  table of contents, sample,
    78-79
staff resistance, 43-44
staff suggestions, 5-19

staff turnover, xi, 37-39
staffing, library, 1
summative evaluation, 108-109
supervisors, immediate,
    checklist, 30-31
  duties and responsibilities
    (NEO related), 29
  evaluation form, sample,
    123-124
  evaluation of neo program,
    120
  initial meeting with NEO
    coordinator, 69-71
surveys, 5-9
  clarity, 8
  demographics, 6-7
  design, 6-9
  field testing, 9
  length/completion time, 8
  rate of return, 9
  samples of staff, 10-13

technology, impact of, vi
tours of library, 90, 92-93
troubleshooting problems, 37-49
turnover, staff, xi, 37-39

welcome banners, 100
welcome letter, 67, 69, 70
  sample for faculty, 70
  sample for staff, 69
welcome packet, 75-76
  checklist, 75-76

Dr. H. Scott Davis is a tenured Librarian and Head, Department of Library Instruction & Orientation at Indiana State University Libraries, Terre Haute, Indiana. His doctorate is in Supervision, Curriculum, and Instruction with emphasis in instructional design, media, and technology from East Texas State University. In addition to administering the library instruction program at ISU and coordinating staff training and development initiatives, Dr. Davis is also team coordinator for a group of ISU librarians actively involved in outreach to academic faculty to provide them with training and instructional support in the navigation of electronic information resources, including the Internet.